DATE DUE

MAY 27 05			

Demco, Inc. 38-293

Myths about doing business in China

Myths about doing business in China

Harold Chee
with Chris West

palgrave
macmillan

First published in paperback 2004 by PALGRAVE MACMILLAN
Houndmills, Basingstoke, Hampshire RG21 6XS and
175 Fifth Avenue, New York, N.Y. 10010
Companies and representatives throughout the world

PALGRAVE MACMILLAN is the global academic imprint of the Palgrave
Macmillan division of St. Martin's Press, LLC and of Palgrave Macmillan Ltd.
Macmillan® is a registered trademark in the United States, United Kingdom
and other countries.
Palgrave is a registered trademark in the European Union and other countries.

ISBN 1–4039–4458–X

This book is printed on paper suitable for recycling and made from fully
managed and sustained forest sources.

A catalogue record for this book is available
from the British Library.

A catalog record for this book is available
from the Library of Congress.

10 9   8   7   6   5   4   3   2   1
13 12 11 10 09 08 07 06 05 04

Printed and bound in Great Britain by
Creative Print & Design (Wales), Ebbw Vale

Contents

List of figures and tables   ix
Foreword   xi

Introduction   1

Myth 1   **One market: 1.3 billion people**   **3**
    Myth   3
    Reality   3
    Conclusion   7
    Box – Go west!   9
Myth 2   **The Chinese market will grow forever**   **11**
    Myth   11
    Reality   13
    Box – China's use of capital   13
    The cost of China's growth   15
    Reforming the state-owned enterprises
    (SOEs)   18
    Box – The mystery of statistics   19
    The labour market   21
    Banking   22
    Conclusion   26
    Box – The enduring legacy of Mao
    Zedong   27
Myth 3   **The market is easy**   **29**
    Myth   29
    Reality   29
    Culturally different   29

	Highly competitive	30
	Bureaucracy	32
	Box – The Chinese as innovators	33
	The legal and regulatory framework	36
	Working capital management	37
	Underdeveloped infrastructure and distribution systems	38
	Labour costs	38
	Corruption	39
	Conclusion	40
Myth 4	**China is Westernising**	**43**
	Myth	43
	Reality	43
	Relationships	45
	Face	48
	Harmony (*hexie/hemu*)	53
	Box – Yin and Yang	54
	The person of quality (*junzi*)	56
	A changing China?	57
	Conclusion	58
	Box – The Great People's Sexual Revolution	59
Myth 5	***Guanxi* is a time-consuming sideshow to the real business of business**	**61**
	Myth	61
	Reality	61
	Box – The king of *guanxi*	62
	How do you attain *guanxi*	64
	When *guanxi* goes wrong	67
	Conclusion	69
Myth 6	**The Chinese are irrationally xenophobic**	**71**
	Myth	71
	Reality	71
	Conclusion	77
	Box – China: the world's oldest surviving culture	77
Myth 7	**The Mask of Fu Manchu: the myth of inscrutability**	**81**

	Myth	81
	Reality	81
	Box – The power of friendship	84
	Chinese culture and context	85
	Chinese notions of space and time	89
	Conclusion	89
	Box – Fu who ...?	91
Myth 8	**Rules are rules: negotiating in China is like negotiating everywhere else**	**93**
	Myth	93
	Reality	93
	Two classics	94
	Box – China: a nation of strategists	97
	The negotiation process	100
	Applying this model to China ...	101
	Conclusion	104
Myth 9	**Chinese business people are not trustworthy**	**105**
	Myth	105
	Reality	105
	Intellectual property rights (IPR)	106
	What can foreign companies do about IPR violations in China?	108
	Box – Right or wrong?	109
	Box – High-tech investment in China	110
	Negotiation practices	111
	Luring the tiger from its lair	114
	Corruption	118
Myth 10	**The Chinese are difficult to manage**	**121**
	Myth	121
	Reality	121
	Box – Power distance in China	123
	Paternalism	125
	Politeness	126
	Fitting in	126
	Cultural bias in Western management methods	128
	Team-working	128

Initiative   129
Feedback   129
Attitudes of Western managers   130
Cross-cultural training   130
Sourcing managers   131
Retaining key local staff   132
Conclusion   133

Afterword   135

Appendix A   A summary of key success factors for
              dealing with the Chinese   137
Appendix B   Some key differences between China and
              the West   139
Appendix C   Making sense of Pinyin   145
Appendix D   Recommended reading   147

Bibliography   149
Index   151

Figures and tables

Figures

1.1	China's projected population growth 1997–2050	6
2.1	Projected GDP growth rates, 2000 to 2020, assuming high and low growth scenarios	15
7.1	High and low context communications	87
10.1	Dilemmas of managing in China	124

Tables

7.1	Key differences in attitudes of Westerners and Chinese	82
8.1	Different perceptions and negotiation procedures	104

Foreword

For people who do not know China and its ways, doing business here can seem terrifying. The rules seem to be totally different.

However, beneath these differences the fundamentals do not change. Business is about providing customers with excellent services or products at a price that they can afford and that makes the provider a profit. It is getting to this point that seems so hard in China.

But it can be done. Novartis has been in China for 17 years and in that time we have established a front-running pharmaceutical company in China, with leadership positions in cardiovascular, oncology and transplantation therapeutic areas.

I have known Harold through his lectures on management and leadership courses, and we shared our views on the changing business scene in China. His book is full of insight of the kind that only someone with his double perspective – of a Chinese person who has worked extensively in China and with Western companies – can provide.

Western readers are advised to read it and use it as a guide to doing business in China. They will find their experience here much more rewarding, financially and culturally, if they do so.

Paul Lau
CEO, Novartis China
Beijing 2004

Introduction

China has always been a land of myth, mystery and exaggeration for the West.

Marco Polo came back to thirteenth-century Venice with tales of cities of a million people (unheard of in those days), unimaginable wealth, exotic food and strange customs. Eighteenth-century adventurers bought tales of rulers enlightened by the wise words of the great sage Confucius. In the last century China became a sinister land full of brainwashed automata brandishing 'Little Red Books'. Now, of course, it is an emerging world economic superpower, 1.3 billion eager consumers and a source of boundless cheap labour.

Maybe the only consistent theme in the West's perception of China has been its inconsistency, or rather a Western desire to see in China what it wants to see. As traveller Stephen King-Hall said back in 1924:

> 'China' and 'the Chinese' are words which embrace so vast a subject that any attempt to set out details inevitably obscures the main features of the subject. ... China, like statistics, can be made to supply apparent proof for any preconceived notion.

Back in 1924, that did not matter overmuch, except to the relatively few people involved in the China trade. But now the problem is serious. In 2003 over $53 billion dollars flowed into China, either in attempts to tap its markets or for some kind of outsourcing.

Sadly, much of it still seems to go astray. Ventures founded with great fanfares end in puzzlement and financial loss. Why?

I have lived and worked many years in mainland China; over this time, I have seen certain misunderstandings and 'myths' emerge again and again in Western dealings with Chinese businesses and consumers. The people pouring this money into China do not understand the place at a deep enough level. Instead they see myths.

The myths vary from the upbeat to the negative. What they all have in common is that they distort the truth. I think they are created out of confusion, in an attempt to answer that most desperate of management questions: 'Why isn't our plan working?'

Yes, China is very different. It is an emerging market with the oldest culture and the largest bureaucracy in the world, with intense competition and an economy that is changing so rapidly that it is sometimes difficult to keep up.

My aim is to remove the myths and look at the truths behind them. These are often truths about culture, a subject often ignored by 'hard-headed' business people. But you must understand culture to succeed in China.

I shall also try and provide guidance on how to deal with the truths behind the myths. The Chinese are as keen as Westerners on mutual benefit, on 'win–win outcomes'. This book is designed to make these more likely.

I have learnt most of what I have written in this book from other people, both in China and Europe: I regret that I am unable to acknowledge individually every contribution.

I would like to express my gratitude to my writing companion Chris West for his contribution, patience and unwavering support during the time it took me to write this book.

I would also like to express my deepest gratitude to Paul Lau for his foreword and to Paul Pinnington for his encouragement and support. I am extremely grateful to Rachel Piper and Lorraine Oliver at the Ashridge Business School Learning Resource Centre, who so graciously scoured the global landscape for every bit of information on China. There are a number of people who have reviewed my manuscript and have provided insightful comments. I want to thank them very much for their counsel and valuable time – they are Barbara Wang, Campbell Thompson, Peng Ningke and Scott Ballantyne.

Harold Chee
Ashridge Business School 2004

Myth 1
One market: 1.3 billion people

MYTH

China is the most populous nation on earth: its 1.3 billion people out-number Europe and the United States twice over. This, of course, is not a myth. But are they 'one market'?

Believers in this myth point to the predominance of the Han ethnic/cultural group who constitute over 93 per cent of the population. Most of them (800 million) speak Mandarin as their first language; for those who do not, over 200 dialects and 80 spoken languages are held together by the same written language. Westerners sometimes find this last fact hard to understand: clearly 'horse', 'cheval', 'caballo' and 'Pferd' can all be represented by a picture, but can whole different languages – prepositions, sentence structures and so on – all be mapped onto the same underlying pictograms? In China, yes. (Or 'yes, well enough', anyway.)

Even deeper is the cultural homogeneity of Han China. Confucian values have reigned supreme for nearly 2,500 years, instilling themselves into every aspect of everyone's life. Even when Communism replaced them, or at least purported to, the homogeneity continued: everyone was subjected to the same barrage of propaganda. (China's great Sage has, in my view, survived this barrage very well, and now reigns supreme again: President Jiang Zemin moved to restore the role of Confucianism in the mid-1990s.) Chinese experience has been amazingly similar, from Harbin to Guangzhou, Lanzhou to Shanghai.

REALITY

None of the above can be denied. Yet it misses the point. Behind this apparently unified façade there is an unexpectedly high level of diversity.

Culturally, climatically, economically, ethnically, geographically, linguistically and socially, China is diverse and complex.

One could hardly expect much else. China is the size of a continent: 3.7 million square miles (9.6 million square km.), the same as Europe. It is 2,725 miles (4,400 km) east to west; 2,500 miles (4,100 km) north to south. Much of China is also mountain or desert, with only 7 per cent of arable land; poor infrastructure exacerbates these already vast physical and cultural distances. From Beijing it takes less time to fly to New York than to reach outlying parts of the People's Republic.

Language is also a bigger problem than the 'myth' leads us to expect. Even Mandarin speakers do not always understand one another. The former Chinese leader Deng Xiaoping spoke with such a strong Sichuan accent that subtitles were added for television viewers. His successor, President Jiang Zemin, gave a speech at the handing back of Hong Kong in 1997 which was televised round China: though people understood it, many viewers found his accent amusing. Almost all national TV programmes have subtitles because of the different dialects used throughout the country.

Even the written language is not uniform. The characters were simplified in the 1950s to boost literacy, but the older forms live on in Hong Kong, Taiwan, Singapore and among the 60 million of the Chinese diaspora around the world.

As one would realistically expect from such a vast country, there are substantial regional cultural differences. A major one is north versus south (of the Yangzi). Northerners tend to be bureaucratic, particularly in Beijing, where government is a major employer and connections in the bureaucracy are an important asset. Their motto for doing business is 'eat first; talk later'. Westerners new to China, or new to *north* China, can become very frustrated with this very quickly. By contrast, southerners – my family comes from Guangdong Province, in the south – have more exposure to business and foreign trade and understand something of foreign business and cultural nuances. Shanghai is particularly entrepreneurial: its people are smart, savvy, ruthless and aggressive, and love to travel abroad. They also pay over 70 per cent of Beijing's taxes! The city is the centre of commerce and finance in China. People living in Hong Kong and Guangzhou (Canton) have historically been involved in international trade: the cities today are China's two biggest ports.

Another cultural split is coast versus inland: essentially, traders versus peasants. But the biggest split of all is between rural and urban. There are really two Chinas: the affluent, modernising cities, especially on the eastern seaboard, and the slow-to-change impoverished countryside, where over 850 million Chinese still live. Their life is traditional, harsh, uncertain and (worst of all for people trying to sell things to them) poor.

It is this divide that gives the lie to the myth of '1.3 billion consumers'. When foreign companies visualise 1.3 billion potential consumers and the prospect of unlocking the collective Chinese wallet, they are struck by 'China Fever' and lose their commercial sense. But what is the reality of this billion-market bonanza?

Approximately 36 per cent of the population (502 million people) live in urban areas. Less than half of these live in the 88 cities with populations greater than 750,000 people. This still amounts to a big market, but it is no longer 1.3 billion.

It is true that there is a drift to the cities. You could even call it a flood. The government has traditionally controlled the rural–urban migration with the *hukou* system of residential permits, but the uneven economic development of the country is putting this system under stress and it is gradually breaking down. The authorities, aware of the desirability of flexible labour markets, are anyway taking a more relaxed approach to this issue. Some people estimate that 50 per cent of all Chinese will live in urban areas by 2010.

Most of these people will still be very poor, however, largely due to the collapse of many of the vast, dinosaur-like state-owned enterprises (SOEs). Income distribution is very uneven in the urban sector, and this disparity will increase as more labour comes in from the countryside. Over time one can expect this to change, but it could be a long time. Maybe not 'long' by the standards of Zhou Enlai (China's premier from 1950–76), who, when asked what he thought of the French Revolution, replied that it was too early to tell. But by the standards of Wall Street ...

In addition to the above, China's population growth is levelling off. This will create a 'bulge' of older people. According to the UN's population projection, China will experience a dramatic ageing of its population: in 2025 it will have about 526 million people aged 50 and above (598 million will be between 20–49 and fewer than 278 million will be below the age of 20). And unlike the West, where many older people have substantial wealth at their disposal, most of the Chinese old are likely to be poor and thus not eager consumers.

The 'age bulge' will also be more pronounced in the cities, where the one-child policy has been enforced more rigorously than in the countryside.

Estimates of China's middle class vary, but a recent report from the Chinese Academy for Social Sciences put the figure at 247 million people. These people earn more than US$5,000 per head, the level at which discretionary (i.e. non-essential) spending takes off. But many are better off than this, as those who work for SOEs have access to subsidised accommodation, healthcare and pension.

To put this in context however, the average disposable income of a US citizen is $25,000 per annum. The US population is 290 million.

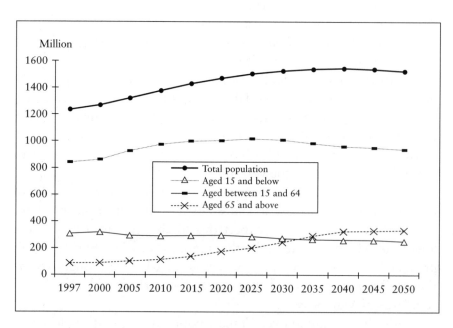

Figure 1.1 *China's projected population growth 1997–2050*

Other countries with average incomes around this level include the pre-expansion European Union with 380 million people, Japan with 127 million and Canada with 30 million. The number of people in China earning $25,000 or more (China's 'gold collar' workers) is about 40 million – still a large market, but not mind-blowing. Not too many companies have gone mad with Canada fever in the last 25 years.

CONCLUSION

Anyone planning to sell into China must find the right way to segment the market. Quite how this segmentation occurs will depend on the product. For food and drink products, the logical segmentation is by cuisine. At its most basic level, China divides into five culinary areas:

- Beijing and northern cuisine is based on wheat and pork: noodles, delicious dumplings, Mongolian hotpot, Beijing duck. (Note: Northerners are also famous for being able to take their drink in bucketloads!)

- Southern cuisine is the lightest, with plenty of seafood and soup. The soup is often cooked with Chinese medicinal herbs, which help to conserve one's vital powers. Dim sum (at breakfast or lunch) is also a southern speciality. Southerners will reputedly eat 'anything with four legs apart from a table, anything that swims apart from a submarine and anything that flies apart from an aeroplane'.

- Western and Sichuan cooking is the most spicy, and can blow the roof of your mouth off. Hot and sour sauce/soup originated in Sichuan, though it is now popular all over China.

- In the very far west, the Muslim Hui people have a central Asian style of cooking, featuring mutton, beef and chicken.

- Eastern cooking, as in Shanghai, Suzhou and Wuxi, tends to be very sweet. Rice and seafood feature a lot.

This is handy information for eating out – but also for launching food-related products. The US sports drinks company, Gatorade, did market research and discovered that consumers in the north of China had sweeter taste buds, whereas southern customers preferred sour flavours such as lime and lemon. They launched different products into these different markets – with great success.

For consumer products, I suggest thinking in terms of four rather different sectors. These are:

- Beijing, Shanghai, Guangzhou, other coastal cities, the south-east

- other cities

- towns

- villages.

You could have a good business serving just the first three cities mentioned, with a population of over 40 million between them and a high proportion of sophisticated and wealthy consumers – but beware: these markets are very competitive. An interesting strategy might be to target a 'second-line' city first, to test the market: somewhere like Xian or Chongqing, or a smaller, coastal city like Dalian ('small' being relative here!).

A market test in one city will probably yield reasonable predictions for other cities, though you will still have to make connections in every major marketplace you enter (more on this later). There will also be local rules and regulations to deal with; China may appear to be a bureaucratic monolith, but it is actually much subtler and more complex than that. This variability is even stronger in rural areas than in the 'first segment', which has been more exposed to Western business.

Anyone still tempted to lump China together as 'one giant market' should spend some time in a small Chinese town, and watch the local TV (there may not be a lot else to do). You will see repeats of films made in the 1950s and 1960s, with an earnest and unworldly tone that would make the relatively worldly, ironic people of Beijing or Shanghai either cringe or laugh. Yet incoming companies still insist on 'national television advertising', unaware of the vast differences between the mindsets of the audiences (based no doubt on their perception of their comparatively homogenous home markets).

A theme running through this book will be of the need to engage with China at a personal and local level. Get used to this idea at once. If anyone tells you grandly, 'I'm going into the China market!', your immediate reply should be, 'Where, exactly?' If they spread their arms and say they are going to conquer the whole place, be very sceptical. If you like them, buy them a copy of this book.

Go west!

The Chinese government has recently emphasised the economic development of the west of China, traditionally poorer than the eastern seaboard, and giving incentives to foreign companies to do business in the area. Most of the projects will be large infrastructure ones: to get into the bidding process you will need to use all the techniques explained later in the book, but the opportunities are considerable.

Myth 2
The Chinese market will grow forever

MYTH

China has been defying economic gravity for a number of years now, confounding the doomsters. This will continue. Labour costs will remain low: there is an almost endless supply of surplus labour out there in the countryside to ensure this. At the same time, a middle class is developing, which will, first, save; second, provide ever-increasing demand for more sophisticated goods; and third, provide ever-improving leadership in both civic and commercial sectors. The government will not back down from its free-market stance, because it knows this is the only way it can generate the ever-increasing wealth that will keep people content (and itself in power).

The data and statistics are stunning. Some examples:

- China has sustained growth rates of around 7–9 per cent over the last 20 years.

- China has been the highest recipient of foreign direct investment (FDI) of all countries – including the United States – since the 1980s, totalling US$57 billion by 2003 (back in 1985 the figure was $1 billion).

- China's economy has doubled in size every six years since the economic reforms began in the 1980s.

- In the last 25 years an estimated 250 million people have been pulled out of poverty.

- Some people estimate the Chinese middle class will number over 500 million by 2020.

- China accounted for about 5 per cent of global GDP growth in 2003.

- China has foreign reserves of over $400 billion, second only to Japan.

- China is currently the third biggest auto market in the world, and the fastest growing. It is expected to be the second largest market in 2007. Volkswagen expects to increase its worldwide sales by 20% to 6 million cars in 2007: half of that figure is expected to come from China. General Motors expects to invest over $3 billion in the next three years in China: not surprising given that, in 2003, the company made a profit of $437 million on selling just 386,000 cars there, compared to the whole of North America, where it made a profit of $811 million on sales of over 5.6 million cars.

- The Chinese economy is already larger than that of France, Italy or Canada, and it is estimated that it will overtake the UK by end of 2005. Arguments rage about when China will overtake the United States (almost all the arguments assume this will happen; the debate is about when). The year 2045 is an average expectation.

- China is the world's largest mobile phone market, with over 250 million handsets.

- Approximately 12 million people a year have been subscribing to China Telecom's land lines over the last few years. For some reason, 2000 was an exception to this: in that year there were 36 million new subscribers.

- After the United States and Japan, China is the third biggest advertising market in the world, with about $6.5 billion spent on television commercials in 2003.

- Wal-Mart imports about $14 billion worth of goods from China annually.

- The Swiss exported nearly $140 million worth of watches to China in 2003.

- China manufactures:

  - over 25 per cent of the global production of colour televisions

  - over 60 per cent of the world's bicycles

  - over 50 per cent of the world's shoes

  - over 50 per cent of the world's cameras.

And so on ...

REALITY

There is a debate about how sustainable this amazing growth is. The drivers of economic growth in China in the last two decades have been: rapidly increasing capital input, due to the high local investment rate and the large inflow of foreign capital; improvements in labour productivity (see box below); re-allocation of labour among industrial sectors and regions; an emphasis on exports; strong domestic demand (helped by lower prices, in turn helped by lower wages, lower taxes and lower cost of capital); and finally an increasing stress on quality and movement up the

---

China's use of capital

World-renowned economist Paul Krugman questions whether there really is much productivity growth in China, and thus whether economic growth is sustainable. This argument has been supported by Chinese economist Wu Jinglian, who said that China makes very inefficient use of capital. In developed economies, $1 dollar of investment yields $1 dollar in increased output, whereas in China the figure is $7 invested for $1 in output. The Chinese economy is only able to sustain this because China has a savings rate of over 40 per cent and can thus afford to go on wasting capital – for a while.

economic ladder – China is today producing high end computers, chips and consumer durables.

Will these factors all continue to operate? Below are two scenarios, one positive, the other less so.

The *continuing boom scenario* rests on the following assumptions:

- China will continue to pursue its reform and open-door policies.

- The global environment will remain stable.

- There will be a continuous transfer of the agricultural labour force to the non-agricultural sectors.

- China's integration into the world markets will continue to deepen.

- Total factor productivity will keep growing at an annual rate of 2.5 per cent to 3 per cent.

The *slowdown scenario* assumes:

- Reforms of the banking sector and state-owned enterprises (SOE) will not be effective.

- There will be hurdles in transferring the agricultural labour force to secondary and tertiary industries.

- Quality of the labour force will improve only marginally and gradually.

- It is likely that the propensity to save will decline.

- Taxes and financial deficits will increase as the government has to increase welfare and social security programmes to compensate for the gradual erosion of family support for dependants.

There is, of course, a third scenario: *meltdown*. Supporters of this scenario argue that the China boom is a bubble, built on fraudulent

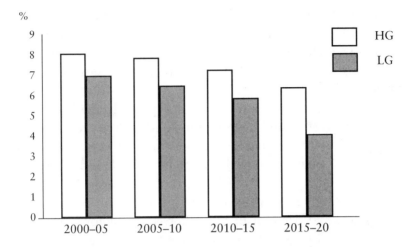

Figure 2.1 *Projected GDP growth rates, 2000 to 2020, assuming high and low growth scenarios*

Source: Development Research Centre of the State Council, PRC 2001

banking practices. Chinese banks are now insolvent and still bleeding money, while covering still hopelessly inefficient industries. There is continued rapid environmental degradation, which will lead to massive humanitarian crises. Income disparity is spiralling out of control ... China is a giant Enron, just about to go pop.

Relax: I don't believe this last scenario. That is another myth. But let us look at the underlying factors in greater detail.

The cost of China's growth

The Mandarin word for crisis is made from two characters, *wei* meaning danger and *ji* meaning opportunity. The interweaving of these two notions should be kept in mind: growth always involves an element of risk. But is China growing too fast, without the necessary controls?

- The country is becoming more aware of *environmental* problems. The destruction has been on a massive scale. In 2001, for example, the Huai River flooded one of China's main grain-producing areas. Flooding has always been a problem in China, of course, but it is now getting worse due to the destruction of forests, over-grazing of pasture land and a multitude of small, ill-conceived dams. Meanwhile some rivers, including the massive and once-destructive Yellow River, have literally stopped flowing in their lower reaches!

According to the environmental expert Elizabeth Economy (2004), environmental degradation and scarcity of resources will drive 70 million farmers off the land by 2025, and the total cost to the Chinese economy will be between 8 and 12 per cent of GDP.

In cities, water supplies are still appalling. In five of China's major cities, 70 per cent of the water is not fit for human consumption, and in only six of the largest 27 cities does the water supply meet the state standards.

In Beijing and Shanghai there is traffic gridlock at most times of the day. Air pollution in many cities is common, and Beijing is believed to have one of the worst rates of pollution in the world. Seven of the world's ten most polluted cities are in China. When I lived in the capital some five years ago, it was quite normal not to see the sun for over a month. At that time the cause was mainly coal burning during the winter, but now this is compounded by carbon pollution from cars.

- There is much less concern for *public safety* in China than in the West, although this is increasing to a small degree in sectors such as the construction industry and the 'sweat-shop' factories in the economic zones.

- *Disparities of income* between city and rural sectors, inland and coastal regions, and between rich and poor have widened substantially. Average per capita urban incomes are three times those in rural areas, for example. Over 50 per cent of the country's bank deposits are owned by the richest 5 per cent of the population. The gap between rich and poor in China is now greater than ever.

- *Agriculture* employs half of China's population, yet produces only 14 per cent of its GDP according to World Bank estimates. The Beijing National Economic Research Institute forecast that 300 to

400 million people will need to leave the countryside. This could take 10–15 years or more to happen, and it is not currently clear that enough new jobs could be created for the migrants.

- *Bottlenecks* are already apparent. Although China accounted for less than 5 per cent of global GDP growth in 2003, it consumed over 30 per cent of the world's steel, 31 per cent of its coal and nearly 50 per cent of its cement. China's oil consumption has risen by an average of 7 per cent a year since 1990: in 2003 the country consumed 5.4 million barrels a day, becoming the second largest oil consumer after the United States (still way ahead at 20 million barrels a day). Currently, China is just about meeting her existing energy needs, but the International Energy Agency have estimated that by 2030 imports will account for 85 per cent of oil consumption. And even now, despite its apparent self-sufficiency in oil, almost two-thirds of China's provinces suffered severe power shortages in the last couple of years. Many factories in Southern China now only have power four days a week and sudden 'black outs' are common.

- Questions are being raised about whether China has the *human resources and competencies* to manage the transition from a planned economy and become one of the super-developed economies. UNESCO estimated that if China is to sustain its current economic growth, it would need about 20 million new university places by 2020. China invests less in education, health and the environment than many of the world's developing nations, so it is far from clear that it will create these university places.

- There is already *overcapacity* in sectors such as steel, car, auto parts and mobile phones. Will this overcapacity lead to price wars, which will in turn affect corporate rates of return and profits, and eventually impact on investment? According to Morgan Stanley, this is beginning to happen, with capacity rising rapidly with a consequent drop in margins.

  The first candidates for the bubble seem to be the car and real estate sectors. According to KPMG, China had the capacity to produce 2.6 million cars in 2003, yet only 1.6 million could be bought by Chinese consumers (KPMG, 2003). They also estimate that in 2005 China will have the capacity to produce 4.9 million cars, when demand will be only about 2.5 million. (The car manufacturers think the overcapacity issue is exaggerated: VW, Honda, Nissan Toyota, Citroen, GM and Ford have all announced further investment in China, reaching a combined total of over $20 billion in the next few years.) The real estate sector will probably be the first bubble to burst. If this happens, it will mean even more bad loans for the banking sector – an issue I will return to below.

Reforming the state-owned enterprises (SOEs)

There is a huge overhang of inefficient state industries, despite the efforts of former premier Zhu Rongji to overhaul the SOEs. These behemoths continue to place a huge strain on other, more productive sectors of the economy. Many are effectively bankrupt, due to poor management combined with an unrealistic burden of social provision, and sometimes also corruption and embezzlement of loans and pension funds by factory managers. It is only now that the issue is being tackled with real resolve. Will this be enough?

Up to the mid-1990s, the state-owned sector employed about 80 per cent of the urban workforce in China. At that point the Chinese government stepped up its efforts to restructure the SOEs, adopting a policy of trying to turn round the large organisations and letting the small ones go to the wall (*zhuada fangxiao*). Their models for the big companies were the Japanese *zaibatsu* and Korean *chaebols*. They have poured resources of funding, technology and training into these businesses – many PetroChina executives have been sent to Harvard, for example – with the aim of creating vast, sprawling conglomerates that will dominate whole sectors of global markets. The jury is out on whether this model is a good one for the twenty-first century marketplace, but at least these companies have been allowed to break half-free of state control, develop corporate governance and raise private capital in the world stock markets.

Tens of thousands of SOEs were at one time owned by central and local government. There are now around 189 very large SOEs, which are controlled by central government under the auspices of SASAC (State Assets Supervision and Administration Commission), and

The mystery of statistics

I should note that not everybody accepts the growth figures put out by regional and national government.

A calculation from Pittsburgh University used energy consumption figures as a proxy for economic growth, and concluded that the true figure was 2–3 per cent lower than the stated growth rates. The Chinese themselves acknowledge that data compiled from the provinces are subject to major errors. This is not surprising, given the historical record of inaccurate measures in Chinese history. During the reign of the emperors, military commanders would not report the true numbers of casualties among their own soldiers, because they feared their heads might literally roll for bringing such bad news.

A modern example of this inaccurate reporting occurred during the disastrous 'Great Leap Forward' campaign in the late 1950s and early 1960s, when China embarked on an ambitious programme of collectivisation, merging small farms into giant collectives and attempting to make them self-sufficient not just in agriculture but in steel. Suddenly China was full of homemade furnaces, into which many useful implements were thrown (you can still see the odd, cone-shaped furnaces, or what is left of them, in remote parts of the countryside). The steel produced was, of course, totally useless, and while everyone was – as ordered – at work producing it, agriculture went to rack and ruin. However party chiefs insisted on getting good figures for output of both agricultural products and steel. Events were held where people competed to announce good results. One of the few leaders to see through this charade, Marshal Peng Dehuai, was later persecuted by Chairman Mao for his honesty. The resulting economic chaos led to a famine that killed an estimated 20 million people. (Most terrifying of all, perhaps, is the fact that no photographic record of that famine exists.)

There is a long and baleful tradition of exaggerating official figures and statistics. I am not saying that Great Leap style deceit is going on now, simply reminding readers to beware of statistics.

15,000 smaller ones. Figures vary as to the number of private businesses in China, but they vastly outnumber these monsters. Many are small, of course.

SOE reforms took on particular urgency when China joined the World Trade Organization (WTO) in 2001.

The restructuring of the SOEs means that the government is abandoning the 'iron rice bowl' of Mao Zedong, whereby the SOEs promised all employees lifetime employment, a pension, and health, educational and social care: nobody was to 'have their rice bowl broken'. This cradle-to-grave provision was admirable in its ambitions, but hardly feasible given the state of China's economic development, especially as there was no link between benefits and productivity or quality of work.

Dismantling this system is a minefield, as many workers are being laid off and made redundant. Many of those have not received redundancy payments or pensions because the SOEs are bankrupt. Protests have erupted in many cities throughout China, especially in the northeast (more on this below), and this has forced the government to slow down the restructuring. However, as foreign competition increases with each passing year, the country's decrepit industrial sector faces ever more factory closures and redundancies. This is political dynamite waiting to explode if the process is not handled skilfully. Failure to manage this effectively will result in increased crime, social protests, even more corruption and a host of other social ills, with China dividing ever more visibly between the haves and have-nots.

However, all is not doom and gloom. The restructuring process is creating some very successful Chinese enterprises that are taking on the global competition. Companies like Legend (now called Lenova) (computers), Haier (white goods), Kelon (white goods), TCL (electronics) and PetroChina (oil/gas) are doing very well in the Chinese market, and appear to be making headway overseas.

The Chinese are very quick at learning and adapting to new situations. They have a highly pragmatic approach to business. Some Chinese state companies are adopting Western management approaches by hiring foreign trainers to give sessions to their people, and hiring foreign talent for their middle management. Some have even gone further, like the Jinjiang Group, one of Shanghai's major state enterprises, who have appointed an American to be

CEO of their hotel division in 2004 and manage their 128 hotels. Even three years ago such a move would have been considered revolutionary: the normal process would have been to appoint a bureaucrat from the government to run the business. (Note that bureaucrats can do a good job; for example the current CEO of Haier has proved extremely successful in turning the company around.)

The labour market

One of China's major competitive advantages is its supply of cheap surplus labour. Many people from the rural sector have migrated to the special economic zones, providing low cost labour for the thousands of factories churning out products for the world market. Manufacturing wages in China average 60 cents an hour, about 5 per cent of the American average and about 10 per cent of rates in some other Asian countries. In this respect, China can and does outcompete many economies in labour intensive manufacturing. But how bottomless is the supply of surplus labour? Pundits have said the answer is 'inexhaustible' – but although there may be 800 million peasants out there, how many are capable of doing the sophisticated work that will be required if China is to move away from low value-added production to the high end of the value chain?

China also needs to create around 15 million new jobs every year just to keep pace with its population growth until 2020. This translates into the economy needing to grow between 5 and 8 per cent per year.

A particular problem is youth unemployment in the urban areas: a government report in 2004 said that about 70 per cent of the urban unemployed are under 35 years old. But China also needs to provide employment opportunities for its 800 million rural population, a third of whom are underemployed or jobless. The government in 2004 has earmarked $1 billion in subsidies for re-employment.

The total of unemployed is set to rise by an additional 25 million in the next few years according to Morgan Stanley economist Andy Xie. This is a vast number even by Chinese standards. Currently, the government figure for unemployment is around 4.7 per cent of the working population, amounting to roughly 30 million people. This figure does not take into account the underemployed. Analysts believe that the true figure may be nearer 15 per cent of the working population. Regionally, the figures are higher in the north-east of China, where the restructuring of the SOEs has contributed to very high unemployment rates, around 25 per cent. The north-east of China embraces the three provinces of Liaoning, Heilongjiang and Jilin, where over half of all SOEs were based. Together, the three provinces comprise around 110 million people, about 8 per cent of the country's population and only a little less than the combined population of Britain and France. This region was the industrial heartland of China during the planned-economy era: today it is a rustbelt. Over a period of five years, 7 million of the 27 million workers in SOEs lost their jobs.

Many protests about unpaid redundancy money and pensions have already been reported. In fact, there have recently been outbreaks of at least threatened violence, with senior managers from SOEs being held hostage by workers demanding payment. (Note that this 'hostage taking' is not just confined to Chinese companies: I am aware this year of a foreign company that laid off workers in China, whereupon some of the expatriate managers were physically held till the workers' demands were met.)

In all such situations so far, problems have been 'resolved', but the very fact that such events occurred raises serious implications about potential social discord.

The government will also have to deal with the estimated 125 to 150 million migrant workers who have left the countryside for the urban areas to seek employment. These people have no welfare payments, health care, housing or schools and certainly no job security. In the three major cities of Shanghai, Beijing and Guangzhou, this floating population constitutes about 30 per cent of their urban population. During boom times, this migrant workforce is a source of economic strength for China, providing low cost labour for real estate constructions, motorways and other infrastructure programmes. In a recession, it could represent a potential crisis, as many of these people are now displaced from the countryside and cut off from the social security they would have had there.

Banking
Perhaps of most concern for Westerners, and the Chinese themselves, is the country's shaky banking system. This is dominated by the big

four state-owned banks: Agricultural Bank of China, Industrial and Commercial Bank of China, China Construction Bank and the Bank of China (in spite of its name, this bank does not have the same function as the Bank of England or the Federal Reserve Bank). Together the Big Four account for more than 70 per cent of lending and deposits in China.

The Chinese banking system is characterised by:

- *Poor regulation.* The Chinese government is taking financial reform seriously, by having reform-minded officials take charge of the China Banking Regulatory Commission (CBRC) to oversee the reforms. But will the reforms be bold enough to make any substantial changes, and what muscle will the CBRC have to enforce its regulations?

- *Easy credit and poor risk management.* Banks need to develop more advanced and sophisticated methods to manage the credits they give to individuals and property developers. Chinese banks have given extensive loans to developers in the highly speculative property market: in 2003, some 20 per cent of bank loans were to this sector. But many development projects never come to fruition; it is not uncommon to see half-built buildings, windowless and with concrete reinforcements still sticking out of the top, abandoned due to a sudden lack of funds.

   Even at the individual level, credit control systems leave a lot to be desired. I know of a couple of individuals in Beijing who were on training courses but not in full-time employment. They wanted to purchase a flat and needed to appear to be employed to get a house loan. They borrowed the deposit, then had a friend who owned a company to make out pay slips in their names. The bank made no check on this: within a week, they were given a loan and purchased one of the new modern flats in the city. We had a very nice party to celebrate.

   In fairness to the banks, mortgage lending is a new business in China and they have little experience in the field, so my guess is that their procedures will be dramatically improved in the future. But will there be enough time to remedy the faults? China, under its commitment to WTO entry, has said that it will allow foreign banks to increase the provision of services to consumers in China by 2007.

- *Corruption*. Only the highest profile scandals involving senior figures make it into the news. The most recent of these involved Zhou Zhengyi, the richest man in Shanghai before his arrest in 2003. As a developer he managed to secure a $230 million loan based on false collateral and manipulation of his company share price. He was able to achieve this because there was a network of corrupt bank officials and the banking system lacked tough credit control systems. The scandal does not seem to have led to any improvements.

   Many SOE officials have access to bank managers and officials who can sanction loans with only a cursory investigation.

- *Theft*. An example of this problem is shown in what happened to a friend's employer, a major multinational company with a Chinese joint venture (JV) partner in Beijing. The Western company took out a Chinese bank loan of about $10 million, partly as a gesture of goodwill to show the Chinese government that it had a long-term commitment to the market. Arrangements were made to repay the loan over a number of years and an account manager was specifically assigned to the company. After 18 months he disappeared with no trace, and the bank said he had died. Then, to the multinational company's surprise, the bank said there was no record of its paying the monthly instalments. Apparently, the manager had absconded with the repayments, leaving no record of payments by the foreign company. Furthermore, the 'dead' manager was later seen by one of the employees of the foreign company walking in central Beijing doing some shopping, presumably from the ill-gotten gains. To add insult to injury, the bank insisted that the foreign company begin repayments from the beginning. Naturally, the company objected and the matter went up to a high level in the political chain, where it was finally resolved, but not without a lot of effort and string-pulling.

   Of course, banks in the West are not immune to such abuse, but in China it is common and occurs at all levels. Gordon Chang gives many vivid examples in his book *The Coming Collapse of China*.

- *Massive bad debts.* According to Chinese figures, over 25 per cent of all the loans by the Chinese banks are unlikely to be repaid in full. This amounts to about $150 billion, but observers such as Nicholas Lardy believe the figure is nearer $500 billion. The staggering scale of this problem is shown if we compare it with the $145–170 billion that it cost the US government to bail out the savings and loans institutions in the 1980s. It is comparable to the estimate of $400 billion of non-performing loans that brought the Japanese economy to a crawl in the 1990s.

- *Excessive dependence on SOEs.* Much of the banking sector's problem stems from the perilous state of the SOEs. The state banks were essentially cash registers for the SOEs, and were used by the government to bankroll them. Lending was not based on commercial but on political criteria – and the lending was massive: in 1998 around 90 per cent of all Chinese banking loans went to the SOE sector.

  The start of reform made things even worse: ministries 'asked' the banks to give financial aid to SOEs to help them pay welfare benefits and pensions to workers who were laid off as a result of restructuring. The SOEs turned out to have no reserves to finance these, as corrupt managers had siphoned off money for into their own accounts. These are everyday stories in the Chinese press.

The government is presiding over various financial initiatives to solve the debt problem, such as providing financial bailouts to some of the four key banks. The most recent initiative is an injection of $45 billion dollars, on top of a previous $200 billion. The aim is to restructure and re-capitalise the banks, to assist them in a future flotation, although the new injection of funds does not allow the banks to use it to write off non-performing loans. The objective is to get foreign capital to buy stocks in the Chinese banks to alleviate the debt crisis.

Pessimists say it is too little, too late. Will anyone invest in these leaky vessels?

Two rays of hope exist. The first is that the Chinese are fanatical savers, and have nowhere to put their savings except in one of these big banks. So deposits are healthy and rising.

The other is time. The government hopes that continuous economic growth will gradually solve the bad debt problem. This is plausible and possible, so long as growth rates are sustained at 8 or 9 per cent per year.

It is also fortunate that few of the debts are in foreign currency: if China's growth slows and the currency depreciates, at least the debts will shrink (in terms of foreign money) with them.

Nonetheless, the situation is precarious: should there be a bubble in real estate or even automotive sectors, this will put real strain on this already troubled sector.

CONCLUSION

Which of the three scenarios do I support? Perhaps rather dully, I cannot see either of the extreme scenarios coming to be. A continued, unbroken march into a bright future looks great on one of those old Maoist posters, but there are clearly too many problems for this to be a reality.

At the same time, I cannot see a 'great crash', 1929-style, occurring. Even if things do go badly wrong, we have a much better understanding of macro-economics than people did in 1929. But most of all, if China falls into a hole, the Chinese will work their way out of it, whatever it takes. China has always fought back from natural disasters, battling to recover from floods, civil wars, pestilence, more wars, famines (and so on). Now, with Western technology and investment, we have the means not just to fight back but to move ahead to prosperity and comfort. Nothing will stop the Chinese doing this, believe me.

China has already weathered two potentially damaging blows. After Tiananmen in 1989, doomsters said it was finished: nobody would trade with China and it would revert to being a sulking, self-obsessed monster, a kind of giant North Korea. This did not happen. Then in the late 1990s, economies started crashing all over Asia. The doomsters smiled again, rubbed their hands and said 'wait for the big one: China will be next'. China wasn't next.

What I think will happen will be growth, punctuated by a series of hiccups prompted by 'mini-crashes'. There will be bubbles in some sectors, and these will have adverse consequences. I am particularly worried about the banking sector. If there is one thing that inclines me to fear for China's future, it is a glance across the China Sea to Japan, where a once-vibrant economy has become enmired in the consequences of unravelling a corrupt banking system. But Japan has only stalled, not crashed, and it has stalled at a relatively high level of prosperity.

The logical consequence of this is that you must choose which sector to invest in. If there is looming overcapacity, avoid it.

If your interest in China is outsourcing rather than serving the local market, 'mini-crashes' will not affect you. They might even help you keep labour and other costs down. The scenario that could cause things to go wrong for you, a complete collapse into anarchy, is not in my view likely. Continue to have confidence!

In the end, I have boundless faith in the energy, determination of the Chinese, in our entrepreneurial nature and, very important, our fear of poverty and pride in our international status. The economic ride may be rougher in the future than it has been in the last two decades, but in the long term growth is here to stay.

The enduring legacy of Mao Zedong

Chairman Mao won't go away. You may see a picture of him on the dashboard of your Beijing taxi or, if you are driving across town, you may pass his giant portrait on Tiananmen, the gate of the old Imperial palace. People may quote him: many of his maxims have entered the speech of educated people.

China pessimists look at the continuing respect for Mao with alarm. Underneath its new capitalist veneer, they say, the country is just waiting to embrace collectivism again. A financial crash will collapse the current system, then watch Mao's admirers grab back power!

They should not worry. Mao is not admired for his politics, but for his achievement in unifying China, founding the People's Republic and standing up to the rest of the world. And, even more simply, because he was a man of power, an emperor. In China that commands reverence. Your taxi driver with his picture of Mao on the dashboard is not a covert Communist: he is more likely to be an entrepreneur.

Myth 3
The market is easy

MYTH

China's decision to open up its markets has attracted Western companies in droves. Everyone seems to be setting up expensive offices in
Shanghai and Beijing; airlines fly daily to China with business class
cabins full. China is hosting its first Formula One race this year
(2004), the Olympic Games in 2008 and the World Exhibition in
2010. All you need is a good idea, several million dollars in capital
handy and a ticket to China. Your products have been a success in
home or similar export markets: China must be next ...

REALITY

China's business environment is unique, brutal and full of unex-
pected surprises. It can be irrational and eccentric in nature. China
is certainly not a 'get rich quick' market or one for the faint hearted.

Few newcomers to the Chinese market have made much money
when compared with the amount of investment they have put in. In
fact, almost no companies have made serious money, and those that
have done have been established in China for many years. In absolute
terms, foreign company earnings in China remain disappointingly low.

China does offer exciting growth prospects, however. In this section I
shall describe some of the key characteristics and peculiarities of the
Chinese market, which may hinder or help foreign businesses operating
in such an environment.

Culturally different
China really is different culturally. Hence my dedicating special chapters

to key cultural notions such as *guanxi*, 'face' and so on; these chapters follow.

Highly competitive

The Chinese market is already highly competitive. As everyone wants to be in that market, a large majority of the global players are already here. And local Chinese competitors are not taking this lying down. Chinese manufacturers had no benchmarks in the old days, so may have seemed able to produce only shoddy, tenth-rate products. Now they are well aware of Western standards and methods, and are perfectly capable of matching and using them, just as Japanese manufacturers were in the 1960s and 1970s. And they are pursuing market share vigorously.

China's market is also dynamic, with consumer loyalty still developing: consumers are still experimenting, and brands come and go with great speed. This does mean that if you get it really right you can establish a fantastic market position. But if you get it wrong, consumers will be off in pursuit of the next promising brand.

When multinationals originally went into China with well-established reputations and brands, Chinese consumers were curious and wanted to buy. Many soon dominated their segments and did so with high margins. But today, Chinese companies have conquered many of these sectors back. Some of these companies, such as Lenovo computers, Haier and TCL, did not even exist 10–15 years ago. Until the late 1990s, for example, the Panasonic brand dominated the Chinese television market, but by 1999 the top five best-selling TV brands were all Chinese. The same goes for the microwave oven sector, which used to be dominated by South Korean companies like LG and Samsung and Japan's Matsushita. Galanz, a Chinese company, now rules the sector with around 60 per cent market share.

In the mobile phone sector, Motorola established itself in China in 1987. China is now the company's second largest market, accounting for about 15 per cent of group sales, with revenues of about $5.7 billion in 2003. It has a market share of 20 per cent. But Motorola is now facing stiff competition from Chinese handset producers like TCL and Ningbo Bird. Overall, the total number of mobile phone makers in China has risen to around 40, producing over 800 models. It has been predicted that in 2006 production capacity will be 200 million.

Of course, there will not be demand for 200 million handsets in 2006 (the most optimistic estimate is 100 million), so the sector will probably be plunged into a price war, with a consequent impact on the margins. How will Motorola fare in such a battle?

It seems that the foreign multinational companies, despite their resources and experience of global markets, are failing to understand the difference between buyer aspiration and effective demand. Yes, we have China's astounding economic growth coupled with the rise of a savvy middle-income group. But the array of goods and services available is simply out of proportion to the segments which can afford them: it has been estimated that less than 10 per cent of Chinese consumers have the level of disposable income that can afford to buy Western products.

'Experts' predicted growth for many types of consumer products, but it is only the mid- to low-end segments that have taken off. For example, in 1993 only 1 per cent of Chinese consumers had microwaves. Consumption grew – but not in the pattern expected. By early 2000, nearly 90 per cent of the market was in cheaper models, with the Chinese company Galanz dominating. There is a similar story with PCs, where in the last few years China's dominant computer company, Lenovo (formerly called Legend), has come to rule the computer segment, with about 40 per cent. The nearest foreign rival is Dell Computers, with less than 10 per cent market share.

The first lesson is that foreign companies should not transplant their global pricing strategies to China, but offer competitive prices (not necessarily the absolute cheapest) in combination with strong brand reputation. Kodak and Fuji films are a good example: both companies charge about 50 per cent more than their local competitor, but less than they do in developed countries. Between them, they have 90 per cent of the Chinese market.

Some foreign technology companies have aggressively reduced their prices to almost Chinese levels, and this has deterred local competitors from entering the sector.

The second lesson is that the Chinese are not afraid to compete head on with foreign companies. Chinese companies will produce their own brands at low cost first, then gradually develop very strong brand positioning. Chinese companies are certainly spending on brand building: according to Nielsen Media Research, only two foreign brands were ranked among the top ten most advertised products in China (Procter and Gamble's 'Crest' and 'Safeguard').

China already has strong national brands; examples include the companies we have mentioned above, plus Tsingtao Beer, Changhong televisions and White Rabbit sweets.

Will Chinese companies develop global brands to rival Toyota or Heineken? Some argue that Chinese companies lack the innovative skill required, but I would not take my eye off the ball here. Smaller, more entrepreneurial companies can and will come up with some nasty surprises for the large foreign multinationals.

Some Westerners argue that the Chinese somehow lack innovative and entrepreneurial skills. They point to the stifling bureaucracy and quota-led production of the Mao era. They would be wise to look at the history of Chinese invention before making such generalizations...

The final lesson is that if foreign companies find their niche under attack from local competitors, they must continuously develop R&D *in the China market* and produce a compelling product at competitive prices. This no doubt explains the recent rush of technology companies such as Motorola and Alcatel setting up R&D facilities in the mainland.

Bureaucracy

I do not claim to understand the total complexity of the Chinese bureaucracy and its machinations. Nobody does, and nobody could – which is precisely why there is no substitute for personal contacts with the relevant authorities (more on this later). What I can do in this section is to give a broad sketch of how government can affect the operations of foreign companies in China.

The Chinese government plays a key role in pursuing China's economic interests both domestically and internationally. It will continue to do so in future, by changing legal and commercial regulations where most appropriate. With entry to the WTO some of its freedom has been lost, but the government is smart.

The Chinese government wants to lay a foundation for a culture where both Chinese and foreigners can make money, and to this end it has embraced reform with a vengeance. In return for allowing foreigners access to China's potentially huge domestic market, massive infrastructure projects such as the Three Gorges Dam and low-cost

---

The Chinese as innovators

China's history of innovation is unparalleled. In China:

- *The compass* was developed in a basic form more than two millennia ago, and in a more refined version in the eleventh century. The first Western use was in the thirteenth century.
- *The decimal system* was used in China 1,000 years before it was adopted by India, from whom the West learnt it.
- *Gunpowder* was developed around 250 AD; it was introduced to the West in the Middle Ages.
- *Silk* was first made around 1200 BC. The West did not make silk till around 1400 AD.
- *Paper* was made from linen scraps in 200 BC.
- *Porcelain* was perfected during the Song dynasty (960–1279).
- *Printing* in the form of effective block printing was invented by Bi Sheng in 1040. Movable type had to wait till 1314. Gutenberg's bible was printed 150 years later.
- *A seismograph* (or at least an earthquake-detecting device effective over a range of 500 miles) was built in 132 AD.
- *The first accurate calculation of Pi* (to 7 decimal places) was made as long ago as 450 AD.
- And so on …

Yes, patriotic Chinese will also come up with 'we first invented the computer' and produce an abacus, but the point must be taken. There is a long and powerful tradition of technological achievement in China. If for various reasons, that has been lost, it has not been lost permanently – just mislaid.

---

labour, the government is seeking new technologies, the transfer of capital and management know-how, and to develop and strengthen the country's external sector. It will achieve its ends, I am sure.

The continuing role of government creates an anomalous situation (by Western standards) whereby the government is not only a player (via the SOEs), but also the regulator. The cards are stacked against the foreign investor and private Chinese companies.

There are a number of characteristics of the Chinese bureaucracy that can make life difficult for any foreign company. The first are the *constant changes* that take place. Regulations are forever altering; new ministries or government commissions are set up; reporting relationships between government departments (and even within them) change day by day. All this fluidity makes it difficult for companies to develop forward planning – even if they are informed of the changes (and usually they are not). Companies must keep a permanent eye on official developments and always be thinking about how these will affect their operations.

A second key characteristic is the *structure of political power within the bureaucracy*. To make it to the top of the power structure requires not commercial acumen but good political skills. Officials' inner, political agendas will always remain primary. One result is that central government initiatives on business can be blocked at local level, as the local official has his/her own plans for the locality and (most important) for him or herself.

The Chinese government has considerable, and by Western standards *arbitrary, powers* to effect changes in the economic landscape. It can decide whether a specific project gets the go-ahead; it can withdraw licences when a project is under way. Government intervention occurs especially when the project is a 'pillar industry' or is visible because of its size, location or the people involved. This arbitrariness can of course be used to advantage. Kodak, for example, was able to develop a way round the laws preventing foreigners from entering the retail sector, not by flouting the law, but by using a particular and ingenious interpretation of it. This cleverness would have come to naught, however, had it not been for the excellent relationship between the CEO, George Fisher, and former premier Zhu Rongji.

The government also has a lot of *informal authority* to match its formal power. It can 'persuade' a company to take a course of action without needing to use its formal muscle. This is consistent with the Chinese philosophy of arriving at a 'mutually convenient' solution for both parties and thus avoiding confrontation. A foreign training company I worked with wanted to run MBA-type programmes in China. The ministry involved in the negotiations 'suggested' that they pursue programmes that did not involve degree-awarding powers. The advice was accepted by the management of the company;

although it was not consistent with the company's vision at the time, it allowed them to fight another day while they continued to unravel the mysteries of the Chinese system. In my view they were right to do so.

As I have already hinted, the best way to circumvent the government's dictates is to develop powerful relationships with the relevant ministries, especially if your business involves government-based projects in areas such as infrastructure development, mining or energy. More on this later.

In the past few years, the Chinese government has begun a process of devolving power to *regional and local governments* in areas such as tax collection and infrastructure development decisions. At the same time, central government still retains oversight of many aspects and has the right to reverse some policy decisions. This decentralisation has further complicated matters for foreign companies operating in China. The bureaucracy has never been homogeneous in the first place, and the devolution of power has exacerbated the potential for confusion.

For example, I know a foreign company that applied for a licence in China and had to deal with four different ministries, each with their own agendas; as a result, it took over three years to get what they needed.

It is not uncommon in very large technical projects to have at least ten or more different branches of the bureaucracy involved.

A further implication of decentralisation has been a power struggle between the centre and the regions. This is particularly evident in recent times when Beijing wants to implement various WTO agreements throughout the country. It is here we see the *realpolitik* of WTO implementation, whereby the provinces drag out the process in order to protect local employment and vested interests.

The decentralisation of power and functions has given local officials tremendous economic power, with the result that different provinces and officials will pursue their own different agendas. This has opened the door to corruption and abuses of power. The many laws and regulations that have been passed are often vague, giving the bureaucrats huge interpretative powers. This has often led to inconsistent enforcement. An example of this is the law that requires permission from the Public Security Bureau for any colour photocopying.

The reason for such a stringent requirement is to deter fraud, especially the copying of important government documents and money (there have been cases in rural areas where peasants have been defrauded by photocopies of money). In some cities, this requirement is rigidly enforced; in others it is very lax and people seem to be able to make copies as easily as in the West.

This variation in enforcement procedures from province to province can be perplexing, annoying and confusing, but that is currently how things are done in China.

All of this means that it is imperative for foreign companies to cultivate relationships with those in government on many levels. Failure to develop *guanxi* (roughly, relations of trust, see Chapter 5) at all levels can lead to major problems. I am aware of a foreign company which developed the appropriate relationships at the national level but not with local officials. So when the factory was completed in one of the provinces of China, the electricity and water were not switched on, even though the factory was ready to operate. These services were only provided once local *guanxi* had been set up – six months later.

The legal and regulatory framework

The Chinese legal and regulatory landscape is still rudimentary and constantly changing. This is understandable, given that the country had no formal legal system in the Western sense until 20 years ago. For example, there are no comprehensive bankruptcy laws to protect businesses, and it was only in the National People's Congress in March 2004 that the principle of private property was enshrined in the Chinese constitution.

Of late, there has been a torrent of legislation, but much of it lacks clarity and is therefore subject to different interpretations. Another weakness is the poor enforcement process. For example, there is stringent intellectual property rights (IPR) legislation in the Chinese Statute books now, but so far little of it has been enforced (more on what you can do about this later).

In practice, some laws are seen as 'more important than others'. Even Chinese lawyers are not always entirely sure or clear about which regulations matter when doing business. Exceptions can always be found for almost any given regulation: as the saying goes in China, 'Things are never black or white, only shades of grey'.

The speed of regulatory change confuses Chinese as well as foreigners. For example, my partner recently applied for a Chinese passport. She went to the application bureau, and was told she needed to collect a new set of documents from another bureau, which she did. She returned these, and was told she needed a stamp from another bureau and a letter from her Neighbourhood Committee (and so on ...). Each step in this process required a journey on gridlocked public transport as the bureaux were in different parts of Beijing, plus the mandatory several-hour stint in a crowded waiting room before gaining access to the relevant official. All in all, the process of getting the correct paperwork assembled and correctly filled in took a week of her time – not just waiting but actually working at the process.

One point of this story is the simple opacity and sluggishness of bureaucracy, but it also revealing that my partner, a bright, aware Beijinger, was not able to find out how the system worked until she was plunged into it – because the system itself is forever changing.

A classic example of this sudden reinvention of rules is the sudden banning of direct marketing in 1998, which pulled the rug from under the feet of companies such as Amway, Avon and Mary Kay. A further problem is that internal regulations usually exist which organisations are expected to follow, but which are never directly communicated to foreign companies.

All this creates an uncertain environment for foreign businesses and it will take at least 10 or 15 years to resolve. Some observers are less sanguine: Donald Clark of Washington University compared China's current legal system to that of the United States in the 1920s. Will China need 80 years to catch up?

Working capital management

In China selling is one thing; getting paid is another. Many companies find huge amounts of working capital tied up with their clients. Chinese customers across all sectors will want some form of trade credit and, depending on their bargaining strength, will get it. It is not unusual to give credit extending from 90 to 120 days: one company I worked for in Beijing often had to wait nine months for payment. This was not regarded as remarkable.

Rural sectors cam be even worse; one company I know found its local distributors demanding not only credit but help with promotion, while returning all unsold goods and not paying one cent for the whole process. This is not so uncommon as one might think.

This is fundamentally a cultural problem. In many cases suppliers did not expect to get paid until the finished goods were sold to the ultimate consumers.

What can you do to get round this? At the most basic level, expect it. Factor it into your plans. Other potential ways round the problem include:

- offering huge discounts for early payment

- using all your *guanxi* (see below) to put pressure on the late payer

- not supplying a second batch of goods until you receive payment for the first one.

But there is no easy answer. Slow payment is a real nuisance in all areas of Chinese business.

Underdeveloped infrastructure and distribution systems

China's distribution systems are vastly different from those that exist in the West. They are underdeveloped and regional in character. This should improve as China's infrastructure gets better, but watch out for problems such as provincial governments charging fees for goods crossing their borders.

Distributors and other intermediaries have high wastage rates, are small, lack capital and have hidden commission systems. It is rare for wholesalers in any industry to have a broad geographic coverage.

Currently, there is a strong European and Hong Kong retailing presence in China, with companies such as Carrefour (France), IKEA (Sweden), Makro (Holland), Metro (Germany), U2, Giordano and Watsons (all Hong Kong). The American and British presence is not as extensive, though Wal-Mart have just opened a large outlet in Tianjin. Under WTO rules, China will need to open its retailing sector even more by 2006.

Labour costs

Companies from economies with rising wage costs like the EU, Japan, Taiwan and Hong Kong are moving their production capacities to

China, attracted by the seemingly bottomless supply of cheap labour. (True, their decisions are further helped by the Chinese government offering packages of incentives such as special economic zones and tariff import reductions, but it is the cheap labour that is the real magnet.)

But low-wage labour is only relevant for industries that require relatively unskilled workers. The reality is that foreign companies setting up in China also need a cohort of highly skilled labour. This is where the problems begin. Although China is producing highly qualified labour, it is not producing enough. So companies end up getting skilled labour from outside the country, hiring financial and computer experts from Taiwan, South Korea and similar countries to work in China at salaries that are almost twice their home rates.

Not only does this prove costly, but it entails cultural and competency issues which are often overlooked – more on this later.

The long-term solution, of course, is 'localisation': hiring locals to replace expats at the middle and upper management levels, but this too can be problematic. I talk about these issues when addressing a later myth, that Chinese staff are 'hard to manage'.

Corruption
This is such a thorny issue that I have given it its own section: see Myth 9.

Along with the above difficulties, there is a further problem that companies face in the Chinese market: their own lack of focus. I have seen too many companies who have caught China Fever and charged in without asking enough questions. What do you want from China? What route do you want to take, and how long is your time-frame? Is China to be your manufacturing base, your outsourcing base, a potential consumer market, or a combination of these? If so, what combination? These questions sound obvious, but I have talked to enough foreign businesspeople in China to know that they are not always asked.

Looking at the options, China can be:

- A *manufacturing base* where companies can have their low cost manufacturing footprint. They have their own factories and produce for their global (and, if relevant, Chinese) markets. China is already known as the 'workshop of the world'.

- *A potentially huge domestic market*. Every company wants to be part of this fast and furious growth market in seemingly every product from cement to shoes, from computers to insurance. Growth rates can be astonishing, as in the mobile telephone market, where there are around 5 million new subscribers per month. But, as I have outlined above, it isn't that easy.

- *An outsourcing base*. In such cases, companies do not own their factories in China but simply outsource their production to local Chinese or joint venture outsourcing companies. For example, General Motors spent $1.1 billion on parts from China in 2003; General Electric has indicated that they will outsource over $5 billion by 2005; Ford aims to have over $10 billion worth of outsourcing by 2010. Wal-Mart already import over $14 billion of goods annually from China. Nike produces 40 per cent of its footwear in China. Etcetera, etcetera ...

Many US and EU companies direct their China outputs to the domestic Chinese market. Yet, this is where local companies still dominate. In the industrial goods sector, Chinese companies control 85 per cent of domestic demand. Even in the transport and machinery sectors, the Chinese still have about 75 per cent of the market. In contrast, overseas Chinese businesses target their outputs to the global market place. This seems a much better strategy.

CONCLUSION

Initially, you must take on board that although the Chinese market may look easy, it is actually not so. The key thing to understand is that you will not be able to tackle it alone (this is as true for a multinational as for a smaller company). You must get the best help you can, developing relationships with intermediaries whom you trust. There is no way round this, much as people schooled in the objective 'science' of business may wish there were.

What kind of help do you need? Many companies entering the China market hire a 'business consultant'. This term can lead to misunderstanding, summoning up pictures of big companies like PWC or Accenture (who do of course, operate in China, and do call themselves consultants!) The kind of consultant I have in mind is more an intermediary, who will help you find customers, get round bureaucrats and create other useful contacts for you.

How do you find such a person? Undoubtedly the best way is via personal recommendation. Do you have a Chinese friend who can advise you? If not, start searching here in your home country by attending as many conferences about business in China as you can. As I hope I am showing, China is not a market you can just walk into alone; the more you meet other people trying to do the same and make good contacts among them, the better. Find a few fellow 'merchant venturers' whom you trust and like, and swap tips, information, contacts.

At the same time, make use of official lists, contact schemes and so on. For UK readers, the Foreign Office used to run an excellent outfit called the Great Britain–China Centre. This combined cultural and business links with an excellent library where you could sit and read *China Daily*, accounts of Victorian adventurers in China, Maoist propaganda, the latest economic and political journals – anything and everything associated with the Middle Kingdom in English. Sadly it has been scaled down, victim of a government cut (and of a current, foolish fad for closing down small, specialist libraries and replacing them with giant, general ones). It has now been merged into the library of Sheffield University, who I am sure will look after it well, but it will not have the same atmosphere – the GBCC staff would make you a cup of tea and chat about their recent visit to Lanzhou or the time they met Deng Xiaoping.

The British Department of Trade and Industry (DTI) has a library, but it is not as wide-ranging as the GBCC one. You need to make an appointment to visit: call the DTI on 0207 215 5000. Business advice on China can also be obtained from the GBCC's de facto replacement, the China–Britain Business Council: visit their website on www.cbbc.org or call 0207 828 5176 (but be prepared just to be referred to the website!).

Also for UK readers, the Royal Institute for International Affairs at Chatham House runs a number of seminars on China; the people on its Asia desk are knowledgeable about China, and the seminars are good places to network.

Incidentally, while I am on this topic, UK readers should not spurn their local Business Link, which can put them in touch with an excellent service run jointly by the DTI and the Foreign Office, called UK Trade and Industry. They can provide a great deal of information, much of it free or at highly subsidised prices.

In China, British and US citizens should contact the British or American Chambers of Commerce. Citizens of every country should contact their embassy in Beijing, who will often have good commercial contacts.

Incidentally, there are now many Western people setting themselves up as consultants on China. (A recent law allows foreigners to set up their own businesses in the mainland, whereas before they would have to create joint ventures. These companies – currently limited to the consultancy and training sectors – are called Wholly Owned Foreign Enterprises, or 'woofies' for short. One hopes that not too many of them turn into dogs.) These are people who have worked there for a while; they know the market; they have contacts. If you know and like such a person, they will no doubt be of help to you, but in my view they are no substitute for a Chinese intermediary. Westerners, however honest, Sinophile and expert, are still essentially outsiders.

You may also need a lawyer for IP protection in China. Do not assume this person will be able to work miracles for you, but a good one can be of value. The process of finding such an individual is no easier than finding the right intermediary. See Myth 9 for more on this topic.

Readers of Chris West's other business books will know that he is very keen on mentoring as a key to success for a new business venture (a start-up or a venture into a new market). This could not be truer than for the Chinese market. Chinese mentors will be invaluable to you to companies that can find them. As with all mentors, make sure you reward them by listening to their advice and keeping them involved in what you are doing.

Apart from making and using good contacts, the great key to success in China is to understand the culture and mores. Which leads nicely on to the next myth ...

Myth 4
China is Westernising

MYTH

Take a walk round Beijing or Shanghai and you are in a Western environment. This is the future of China!

REALITY

China uses Western technology, and often wears a kind of Western mask (e.g. people in suits, documents in English). There is widespread adoption of Western ideas, fashion, music, management techniques and so on. This is perceived by many as proof that China is Westernising, but look at what is going on behind the scenes, and you will see *China is modernising rather than Westernising*. Underneath it all, there is still a strong and deep-rooted culture based on Chinese values. A good example is provided by modern Chinese weddings, where couples wear Western clothes but strictly follow traditional Chinese procedures. The bride in her flowing white Western dress and the groom in his suit or morning coat will still bow to heaven, earth and then each other at the start of the ceremony. The bride and groom will serve tea to their respective parents and red packets of money will still be handed round. The ceremony has not changed for hundreds, maybe thousands of years.

China's 'Open Door' policy (1978) was to reform its economy, but not necessarily in terms of the West's liberal market structures. The aim was to create 'market socialism with Chinese characteristics'. In line with Chinese notions of time (see page 89), the government took a cautious and, most important of all, gradual approach, which meant that China's traditional Confucian culture and the legacy of

Communism continued to affect perceptions and behaviour very strongly. Anyone seeking to do good business in China needs to understand both Chinese culture and the Communist influences.

China has always been characterised by its huge size and its need for continuous control of an unruly environment and (thus) of vast numbers of people. Natural disasters were frequent and devastating; the 3,000 mile-long Yellow River (Huanghe), for example, has changed its lower course several times in history, causing massive flooding and many thousands of deaths. Mastering forces like these was a huge project entailing vast gangs of labourers, themselves in need of powerful, unquestioned, central control.

These disasters also produced a profound awareness of scarcity in the Chinese psyche.

China's legal system has always been weak in comparison to the huge task required of it (controlling the most populous nation on earth), hence there has always been a need for a powerful code of personal relationships to supplement it.

China's culture is still predominantly based on the ideas of Kong Fuzi (Confucius). Confucian ethics remain the bedrock of thought and behaviour in mainland China, and perhaps even more so in Taiwan and Singapore: in China, Confucianism was driven underground during the Mao era (there was even a specific 'criticise Lin Biao and Confucius' campaign during the Cultural Revolution). It has become a kind of shadow religion on the mainland, exercising massive influence in all areas of life, but not practised or discussed openly.

Confucius was born in 551 BC and was a wandering teacher, bureaucrat, diplomat and adviser to princes. The system he developed is not a religion but a system of ethics. It is an irony that his ideas were only implemented 300 years after his death, during the Han dynasty (206 BC–220 AD). Since then, however, Confucianism has survived China's turbulent history with extraordinary resilience. Is it fighting a losing battle against Westernisation? Some people claim that it is, but I see little evidence of this.

Confucius based his teachings on the importance of hierarchical relationships. These provided guidelines for behaviour within the inner and extended family and in wider society. Responsibility in traditional Confucianism was first to the ruler, then to one's parents, then to one's teacher, then to siblings and relatives, and finally to friends. (In contrast, a typical Western responsibility hierarchy might be to one's own principles first, then to one's family, then to society.) Chinese social norms are still derived from these ancient and powerful guidelines.

Confucius also focused on respect for tradition and the importance of collectivism, in particular the critical role of the family. It is impossible to overestimate this role in the Chinese mindset. We are passionately focused on our families and close friends, and have been so for thousands of years. We extend the notion to consider being Chinese as being part of a huge family (like all families, there is internal strife from time to time, for example during civil wars, but in front of foreigners, all differences are buried and national – for which read 'family' – unanimity reasserts itself.) This theme will occur again and again throughout this book: apologies if I 'overstate' it, but it intrudes into all areas of Chinese thought and feeling.

Confucius' teachings were neither democratic nor individualistic, but dedicated to the principles of harmony and stability. He had little time for law, arguing that what mattered was the quality of the ruler. If the ruler was a person of quality (*junzi*, see below), good government would follow naturally – the 'rule of man' and not the 'rule of law'. The behaviour of some of China's leaders since Confucius' time has shown that to be idealistic.

There are four key Confucian values that anyone seeking to deal with China and the Chinese must understand: relationships, face, harmony and the person of quality.

Relationships

Probably the most important influence on Chinese society has been the Confucian view of hierarchical relationships. These embody social obligation to political authority and to the family. Confucius argued that rules and rituals of these relationships were what held human society together (it is essential to understand from Chinese history that anarchy is felt as a real and terrible threat: every time a dynasty has crumbled and China collapsed into civil war, the strife has been massive and disastrous). The five relationships are:

1. Ruler–subject.

2. Father–son (more broadly interpreted now as parent–child).

3. Husband–wife.

4. Elder–younger.

5. Friend–friend.

The primacy of the *ruler–subject* relationship is reflected in the Chinese attitude to authority, which is, by Western standards, deferential. Younger Chinese today may be rebelling against this, but many still accept a higher level of authority than their peers in the West.

There is a Chinese saying 'be careful, or the leader will give you tight shoes' (*Xiao Xin ling dao gei ni chuan xiao xie*). Chinese leaders can make life very difficult for anyone whose challenge becomes uncomfortable to them. People in China are used to living in the shadow of being given tight shoes.

Obviously this has an effect on business. It is not just about obeying the CEO, but in any group there will be a leader, and others will defer to them. If you do not respect the hierarchy that prevails among the Chinese you are dealing with, you will not be respected by them.

The relationship between *parent and child* also has immense power in Chinese life. The relationship was more complex and subtle than is often thought: an unequal role did not mean unequal obligations. Yes, the child's obligation was more powerful, but the parents owed affection, sustenance, respect and self-sacrifice to their children.

Westerners, especially those bought up from the mid-1950s onwards, rarely understand the power of this obligation.

Here is a traditional Chinese tale I was taught as a boy.

> A warrior leaves his pregnant wife to fight for his emperor, and returns home after 20 years. As he nears his home he sees a young archer shooting at a wild pig and they get talking. This is, of course, his son, but neither of them realises this. The young man challenges him to an archery contest and accidentally the young man is killed.

In this tale, one person has committed two cardinal sins. Who?

Westerners to whom I tell this story come up with different answers. Some say the father, for deserting his wife, for failing to inform his wife he was coming home after 20 years and just expecting everyone to recognise him, or just for being such a lousy shot that he kills a fellow participant in an archery contest. (Silly old fool – he ought to know when his time is up and get out of the way of the younger, fitter man!) Others say the lad, for being a show-off and running unnecessary risk. A third group blames the mother, for not teaching the son enough about his father so that the boy did not recognise him when he appeared. And I've even had 'the emperor' as a reply, for taking a father away from his pregnant wife.

No Chinese would doubt the answer for a moment. It is, of course, the son, because he (a) did not know his father and (b) challenged his father.

Unfair! say most Westerners when they hear the answer. The young lad had never set eyes on the old man – how was he to know? And why shouldn't young people challenge the old? It is the way of nature, and of modern competition: when China enters the Olympics, it does so with its fittest athletes, not a bunch of greyhairs.

I can see their point of view, but the Chinese in me knows the Chinese answer is right.

The Confucian *husband–wife* relationship has often been misunderstood as a kind of charter for exploitation. It is not. The five relationships always involve reciprocal respect, duties and joint submission to higher, collective goals. Many Chinese women are powerful individuals, often behind the scenes but not always. Empress Wu Zetian ruled China very efficiently during the Tang dynasty. In modern China women hold many senior positions. OK, more in human resources and IT than in other areas (but this is exactly like the West). China's representative at the WTO, Wu Yi, is a woman, as was Wu Shihong the former head of Microsoft China. Female executives or female entrepreneurs coming to China need not fear the kind of prejudice they might encounter in some countries. You will be treated with respect, and find that China is a safe country to travel in.

The respect accorded to *teachers* is still strong, which makes teachers' work a lot easier than in the West (and makes life for pupils easier too: they come out of school well educated for life). Chen Kaige's beautiful film *King of the Children* expresses this respect much better than I ever could. When I work in China training managers who have a high social status, I am overwhelmed by the respect that is accorded to me as a result of my position as their teacher.

Face

One cannot understand Chinese behaviour without an understanding of the concept and role of face (*mianzi*). Face is about one's self-respect and prestige and, crucially, about one's standing in the group. It is an essentially public phenomenon, though it has powerful (albeit secondary) emotional consequences. The emotions are about dignity and dignity's enemy, shame. This polarity runs deep in the lives of Chinese people: Westerners, trained to live in a more individualistic society, often fail to grasp the power of these concepts, or think that Chinese, because they rank emotion behind public appearance, somehow 'don't feel strongly'. We do.

Face is a key component in dynamics of *guanxi* (of which much more below!): loss of 'face' means reduced social resources to use in cultivating and developing one's connection network. Face is gained by good connections, wealth, power, intelligence and even (in modern China) attractiveness. Face can be likened to a credit card: the more you have in the account, the more credit you are given. But you can extend this too far, 'overdraw on your face' and find yourself in debt. In the long run, the face account needs to be in balance.

It would be difficult to estimate how many people have been toppled from power, or how many friendships been destroyed, over face.

Westerners often wonder why the Chinese make such a fuss about face. Doesn't everyone have some sense of dignity that can get hurt at an insult? Surely the Westerners who descend into feuds about petty things like leylandii hedges are just as overcome by this as 'face-conscious' Chinese? Some visitors wonder if the whole thing isn't a bit of a show, put on to stop Westerners doing inconvenient things like bargaining hard and speaking their mind.

To take such a line is understandable – especially when you have just strayed over some line of Chinese etiquette that makes no sense to you – but very dangerous. Face matters. It is not just about feelings, but a key part of what holds society together. And it is not 'put on'. Even the mighty Communist Party, which initially tried to eradicate it with no success, wisely ended up by adopting the notion for its own ends.

Carl Crow, a writer on China in early 1930s, understood this concept and its importance:

> No one in China is too lowly to treasure and guard his 'face', that is his dignity and self respect. And no foreign resident has ever accomplished anything in dealing with Chinese if he failed to take this factor into account. Those who know how to utilize it have found life pleasant and sometimes prosperous.
>
> (C. Crow, *400 Million customers*, 1937)

Note 'pleasant and *sometimes* prosperous': Crow also understood Chinese business!

Okay, so what can we learn about it?

- Face is a dynamic concept: one can give, receive, save or lose 'face'.

- Face is so important that it justifies spending money even if you have little of it. For example, young Chinese girls are prepared to live extremely frugally day-to-day, and yet to splash out for imported make-up, designer clothes and so on. Other examples are people who entertain at restaurants that are both lavish and expensive even when they cannot afford it, and new businesses that rent prestigious, expensive premises in apparently inappropriate locations.

- Westerners often see the above as silliness, vanity or showing off, but this is simplistic. Face is not about oneself (in a self-regarding way; the modern slang term for this might be one's 'ego') but about one's *social* role. The outer display of apparently 'wealthy' Chinese is only specific to a role they are supposed to play, which in turn gives them face. On their own, individuals count for nothing (a tenet shared by Confucianism and Communism). Individuals are expected to be humble about themselves, but allowed to be forceful about their social roles. This seems 'inauthentic' to Westerners, but it must be understood in order to make progress in Chinese society.

- Organisations and countries have face too. Ministries/corporations/bureaux have reputation to worry about: during the communist era, government officials and foreign state leaders would ride in specially built limousines called *hong qi* (red flag) to indicate their importance and the face of the country. (Today, government officials tend to ride in Audi A6 cars.) The Chinese government will do their utmost to ensure that the 2008 Olympics turn out to be the most successful ever.

Face, as I've said, can be lost. Very easily, for the unwitting. Classic ways include:

- Publicly insulting someone intentionally, or even unintentionally, would be an affront to one's own personal dignity (as it upsets harmony – see below) as well as to the dignity of the victim. During the Cultural Revolution in the 1960s, for example, it was an intentional tactic to publicly humiliate those who were perceived to be counter-revolutionaries: in the short term this worked, driving many decent, honourable but temporarily inconvenient people to suicide. In the long term it backfired. People viewed the Red Guards as brash, arrogant and lacking in dignity. It is no accident that those leaders who were 'shamed' in or stood back from the Cultural Revolution, such as Liu Shaoqi or Zhou Enlai, are now the most admired figures of their era (apart from Mao: one does not criticise the emperor).

- Cultural insensitivity or pure ignorance. A personal example: I attended a banquet given by the foreign partner of a joint venture in Shanghai. The president of the foreign company gave a speech, but did not offer the Chinese president of the JV the opportunity to make a speech too. I am sure this was not intentional, but would have been interpreted by the Chinese side as not 'giving face' to the Chinese president (and thus showing that the rude foreigners had no face to give, anyway).

- Declining an invitation to a social or business function on a weak pretext. When I go to China on a short visit, there are many friends I would like to contact for a brief chat. But I know that if I call them, they will invite me to dinner, and that I will not be able to accept because there is not enough time. So I do not get in touch. Westerners may say this is silly, and maybe it is, but that is how things are. If you are in the position of having to turn down an invitation, defer it rather than flatly refuse. 'When I am next in China …' The person will get the message.

Well-connected people can find themselves in the difficult position of being invited to clashing engagements – one Hong Kong businessman I know was invited to five dinner engagements on the same night during the Chinese New Year week! In the West, we usually decline subsequent invitations: 'I'm sorry, but I'm already busy that evening' is an acceptable response. Not in China. He had to attend all five parties, spending less time at each party but thereby both 'giving face' to all his hosts and preserving his own face too.

- Refusing a request. Again, this is a difficult one to get round. Chinese find this difficult too. There is in practice an etiquette about asking favours: you shouldn't ask for extravagant favours from people, because you put them in a position of having to grant them or lose face. This is why trust takes time to build: one aspect of being trusted is that the other person knows you will only ask for reasonable favours or, if you do ask for something big, it will be because you are in truly dire need.

  All Chinese people will have stories about embarrassment caused by difficult requests. Recently, I was dealing with a client company through an intermediary. She wanted me to reduce the price of the package I was offering, because she had 'promised' the other side that this was the end game of the negotiations. I instantly knew that if the price was not reduced – something I was not happy to do – she would 'lose face'. I had to take a long-term view here, and do as she asked: I would have more opportunities later to do more, better business through her.

- Refusing a present. The sender will lose a lot of face in this situation, feeling perhaps that their present is not good enough and also feeling that he/she is looked down upon by the receiver. During the moon festival in August, many moon cakes are given; it would be the height of folly to turn down any moon cakes, even though one has a mountain of the things in the house already! Accepting the cakes gives face to the sender and saves your own face.

- Being too independent. When you are having a meal at a restaurant and one party offers to pay for the meal, under Chinese etiquette it is appropriate to offer to pay too. You then haggle as to who should pay: in the end, your Chinese host should 'win' and pay. Foreigners often find this confusing: used to perhaps one round of haggling back home, they start wondering if they really should pay after all. In reality, you just have to play the game. What you should not do is offer to 'go Dutch'. This would be construed as not giving face to the person who offered to pay, perhaps even indicating you don't want to be close to them, or even an insult, implying that your host cares so much about a little money. (Don't worry – 'China hands' soon get used to the ritual and start to enjoy it.)

- Losing control of yourself by displaying anger, aggression or grief. I have seen expatriate managers lose their temper with Chinese staff: Chinese workers then disengaged from the now shamed managers, who ultimately lost control and authority.

How do you preserve face? Given the diversity and complexity of social situations, there is no simple model. If there were a word to sum up the right kind of behaviour, it would be 'diplomatic'. (Diplomacy is not always encouraged in Western commercial organisations, where straight talking is the preferred way. More on this later.)

Position yourself in a social context so that your Chinese hosts can understand you, by *demonstrating you are part of a network*. When meeting people for the first time, establish some common ground both socially and professionally. This entails giving details of your job position, your company and so on, but also of people you know. In the West this may be construed as 'name dropping': in China it gives both you and your interlocutor face. It also entails asking about the other person and discovering more about them. In a group setting, the smart person notes some fact about every individual, and leaves with a comment to each about that fact, thus giving them all face.

The requirement to reveal your status explains the critical importance of giving your business card when you first meet a Chinese businessperson. Make sure this card has a title on it – 'Vice-President, Sales' – something Western cards sometimes omit in the attempt to appear pally and informal. Chinese will just think you are a nobody! And remember to both give and receive name cards with both hands, which is also a way to show face.

While showing your status is important, it is also important for the group to be seen as the dominant force. 'We agree' carries much more weight than 'I agree'.

If you damage someone's face, what do you do? Third parties or intermediaries are used in both business and personal situations. For example, I inadvertently offended one of my Chinese friends and had to ask a mutual friend to find out why he was cool to my overtures to socialise. Only then was I able to find out what had happened and apologise. Even so, the relationship is not back to where it was: I will have put work in to develop it again.

Chinese people are acutely conscious of the minutiae of 'face', of actions and words that demean – or elevate – another person. Things that in the West we would brush aside ('That's just Rick's way – he doesn't mean it personally – now, let's get on with business ...') are noticed and, more importantly, *felt* in China.

Behind this, of course, can lie a feeling in the Chinese mind that Westerners are either stupid for not noticing these things, crass for not feeling them or rude for not acting on them. The more you can act within the rules of face, the more you can do to dispel this prejudice. Myths exist on both sides of the Western/Chinese interface!

Harmony (hexie/hemu)

The third key concept of Confucianism is harmony. Implicit in this idea of harmony is the concept of balance, which is derived from the Daoist concept of Yin and Yang, two opposite forces that need to be kept balanced over time (one may prevail for a while, but if so, the other must come back and be reasserted). The nearest thing I have found to compare to this in Western thought is the Greek dichotomy between the Apollonian and the Dionysian traditions, one serene and contemplative, the other active and energetic.

The Confucian concept of harmony is based on balance. It operates at both the individual and social level. Socially, it led to an intensely conservative approach, as does almost all traditional

Chinese thought. Personally, the message is more dynamic. Harmony has to be achieved. Once you achieve balance in your life, and only then, prosperity will prevail. My father used to say to me that a harmonious man is one who can achieve the balance in his life of being a good son, a good father, a good husband and having a successful career. Until I had achieved all of these, I would not be in proper balance and therefore not in harmony, so I would not be truly happy or wealthy.

As with many things, the Chinese invented the work–life balance long before the West!

Note the interlinking of Confucian concepts. If a person maintains the *correct relationships* among individuals, this protects his/her *face*

Yin and Yang

The twin concepts of Yin and Yang both figure in the oldest books of Chinese, the *Book of Odes* (*Shi-jing*) and *Book of Changes* (*Yi-jing*, better known in the West as the *I Ching*). The latter is supposed to be nearly 4,000 years old.

The Yin–Yang theory is the most characteristic and pervasive concept in Chinese thinking. The literal meanings of Yin and Yang are the shadowy and sunny sides of a hill, and by extension darkness and light. Yin–Yang represents all the opposing principles we find in the universe. Thus, under *Yang* we have the principles of sun, heaven, maleness and dominance, while under *Yin* we have the principle of cold, darkness, femaleness and submission. Each of these opposites produces the other, so that everything in the world is a mixture of the two: though there is in one sense a struggle between these elements, the struggle is transcended by their interdependence.

Western logic finds it harder to deal with the perpetual co-existence of opposites than Chinese. Even Hegel, whose 'dialectic' was supposed to be less draconian than the Aristotelian 'either/or' logic that the West uses in everyday life, posits an ultimate principle that will finally emerge triumphant from the interplay of opposites. (Marx, of course, followed him.) Chinese logic assumes no such ultimate triumph: Yin and Yang will keep on interacting, the wheel of fortune will keep on spinning round.

> This tolerance of duality affects the way that the Chinese think about business. In negotiations, for example, Chinese thinking would be based on trying to find a situation whereby the outcome would be X *and* Y (a win–win outcome) and not X *or* Y (the zero-sum game all negotiators seek to avoid). This partially explains the protracted negotiation process you will encounter in China.
>
> The *Yi-jing* (*I Ching*) is an immensely powerful book. It is still popular – and used – in modern China, where there is a *Yi-jing* association and a number of *Yi-jing* masters whose advice is in great demand. I use the book myself, often. This may surprise you, given that I am supposed to be rational and am highly educated in logic and science. But, the Chineseness in me still has a powerful pull. The *Yi-jing* can highlight factors that we may not foresee: there are, after all, elements in life which lie outside our range of perception, and in my view the *Yi-jing* can highlight these. Before any major decision, I consult the *Book of Changes*, hoping it will make me aware of issues that have lain outside the scope of my thoughts. (I use coins, not the traditional method of yarrow sticks.) I am pleased to report that many a consultation has thrown new light on things and has led to much wiser decisions.

and that of others. In doing so, that person will preserve social and individual *harmony*.

The concern for social harmony can take many forms. For example, if you are engaged in a conflict with Mr X, before you decide to take action such as suing him, you must make sure that you do not upset any intermediate relationship connected with Mr X and you. Everyone in the Chinese *guanxiwang* (social network) is important: upsetting anyone in the network can lead to destabilising the web of connections. Furthermore, if you make your decision to go ahead and sue, you will need to consider the consequences of this decision with regard to his face and to your own.

I have often witnessed Chinese tell a 'white lie' not for any personal gain but simply in order to preserve general harmony and prevent conflict. This is in no way considered dishonourable – quite the opposite. For example, when people are critically ill, it is customary not to tell them how serious the illness is in order to preserve harmony and peace of mind, and to prevent them being upset and losing their will to fight the disease. My partner's grandmother died without being told the type of disease she was suffering from. From a Western perspective, this may seem abhorrent, but in the Chinese context it is perceived as humane.

The following points will help to illustrate the Chinese attitude to harmony and its link to the notion of face:

- Strong expressions of emotion can disrupt group harmony.

- Public expressions of praise for a particular individual can embarrass that person. Such comments could endanger the social balance by giving the individual greater status than his or her peers.

- Outright expressions of negative emotions draw attention to one's own problem and thus cause loss of face. (In the West this can act as a social bonding process by sharing problems collectively.)

Remember our keyword 'diplomacy'. Praise or criticise in private, or phrase things implicitly. Gestures are worth a thousand words.

The person of quality (junzi)

The original meaning of *junzi* was 'son of a ruler', but it referred to a person's moral character rather than birth: in Confucius' day, only sons of rulers received the education that made one a *junzi*. The person of quality would observe the proper rituals of etiquette in all his behaviour; he (it was a 'he' in Confucius' day) would respect human dignity and cultivate humaneness (another important Confucian concept); he would conduct business and political matters in a fair and impartial way; he would show filial piety and loyalty to the state, his parents, siblings, relatives and friends; he would carry out his obligations to his wife, children (and so on). The keys to becoming such a person were twofold: education and constant self-examination.

Politically, Confucius believed that in societies led by such people (and regulated by etiquette), citizens would naturally develop a sense of morality and conduct themselves properly. Hence his belief in the 'rule of man' rather than the 'rule of law': in a society governed by politics and penal law, people would not develop a sense of shame or morality and would break the laws when it suited them.

How does this fit in with modern day China? 'China-bashers' will say not at all, but it would be unwise to write off Confucian ideals, even if the harshness of life makes them sometimes hard to put into practice. The belief that business relationships should be based on human values (trust) and on rules of etiquette is pure Confucianism.

Education, one key to becoming *junzi*, is still highly valued. When it comes to marriage, many people say a partner is a 'good person' or 'educated' rather than they are beautiful or handsome. (In a survey, actually in Taiwan but it could have been China, students were asked for values by which they would assess potential partners. One of the most important was 'graciousness in speech'. Not surprisingly, this value did not feature at all in a sister survey carried out in the West!)

Self-improvement, the other key, is coming back into fashion via self-help books. This is the reassertion of an age-old tradition that was seamlessly maintained during the Communist era by books like Liu Shaoqi's *How to be a Good Communist* and Chairman Mao's *Little Red Book*. Chinese people still set themselves exacting standards. Built into the culture is notion that you must '*yi de fu ren*': convince people by your integrity and ability. Note that when you start getting close to Chinese people, the same standards will be applied to you.

You may see people arguing in the street in China, but fists are very rarely raised, as to do this would be against the ethic of the *junzi*.

The opposite of *junzi* is *xiaoren* or small person.

A changing China?

A subtler version of the myth we are debating is that China may be neo-Confucian now, but is changing fast as more and more Chinese interact with the West. This book will deny this. Chinese are becoming better at playing the Western game, but fundamentally their values and outlook are unaltered. China is not going to abandon its old ways to suit the West.

Yet changes are happening – so much so, that some Chinese do question how long we can sustain traditional values. The 'little emperor' generation (children of the one child policy) appears to be rejecting many traditional notions, expecting to be 'spoon-fed' even after the age of 21. They are said to be self- rather than family-centred, and to have been spoilt by the 'six parents' looking after them (the child's own parents, plus both sets of grandparents). Economic imperatives are making other Chinese abandon deeply held values: in booming Shanghai, some of the more affluent families are putting their parents into old people's homes – anathema to most Chinese.

Is this the beginning of the end? Most Chinese believe these changes will not be the norm, and quote many examples of overseas Chinese relations who cling to their traditional roots even in a Western setting.

When Deng Xiaoping was questioned whether his opening up to the West would have an effect on Chinese culture he simply commented that, 'If you open a window, one or two flies might enter the room.'

Dr An Wang, the founder of Wang Corporation, put it more elegantly:

> A Chinese can never outgrow his roots. Ancient ideas such as Confucianism are as relevant today as they were 2500 years ago. There is a practical genius to Chinese culture that allows it to assimilate new ideas without destroying old ones.

The changes that will undoubtedly come about in China in the new century will, in my view, reflect Dr Wang's process of assimilation rather than one of cultural destruction.

CONCLUSION

The point of all this is that you must develop a working understanding of the reality of Chinese culture in order to do business in China. Ignorance will earn you contempt and bring about commercial failure, even if you have the most wonderful product in the world.

The Chinese do not expect foreigners to be masters of China's ways, but they do expect a measure of knowledge and respect. This should transcend simple rules about what kind of present to give (though such rules are useful). The aim of this book is to provide an introduction to the social context.

The Great People's Sexual Revolution

China has undergone a sexual revolution in the last few years, at least in the big cities. Officially, the Chinese attitude to sex is still puritan: any pre- or extra-martial sex is disapproved of – which is progress when compared with the bad old days, when many women were put to death for such transgressions (the men often, though not always, got away with it). (Concubinage was a different story. This was effectively polygamy: the concubine was 'married' to the man and lived in the house with the first wife. My grandfather had two concubines, one of whom is alive today: she is my 'second grandmother' and as much a member of the family as anyone. Today, of course, the practice is illegal.)

The generation under 30 is particularly open to outside influences. It is not uncommon in the cities to see young couples holding hands and even embracing quite openly, something that would have been unthinkable a few years back. University students are sharing flats rather than living in the traditional single-sex university dormitories. Younger people who can afford it rent apartments and live together as couples before marriage. Recent research by the Academy of Social Sciences in China said that the proportion of couples engaging in pre-martial sex in Beijing is around 80 per cent, compared with about 20 per cent in the 1980s. These are truly momentous leaps in China's social revolution: foreigners who had not been to China before the 1990s would have difficulty understanding quite how momentous.

For gays and lesbians, things have changed much, much less. Homosexuality is still stigmatised: many Chinese of all ages have an extremely strong negative reaction to it. Please be cautious. Having said this, there are a few gay bars in both Shanghai and Beijing; and a recent Chinese film showed the life of a gay couple.

And for everybody, please note also that there are still many people in the cities who still have conservative values, especially the generation over 40. I would strongly recommend caution in your behaviour so as not to offend Chinese sensibilities.

What has not changed much is the attitude to children born outside marriage (*sishengzi*) and their parents, especially for the mother. Officially, the child will be denied a birth certificate and a '*hukou*' (residence permit). Socially, the sense of shame is enormous: the woman faces ridicule at the workplace. Even parents are often unsympathetic to their daughter's plight, as she has brought shame to the family.

Fathers of illegitimate children? They get off more lightly, often just bunking off and taking no responsibility.

Divorce is not new in China, and occurred even in the Qing dynasty when the empress divorced the last emperor. However, it still carries a stigma. Those who are divorced are perceived to be of 'less value' and in an SOE or governmental setting can suffer disadvantages such as missing out on promotion. In joint ventures or start-ups, attitudes are more liberal. Even here, though, there is still a feeling amongst most Chinese that, given their choice, they would rather not marry a divorced person.

As I said, these comments relate to the cities, and probably only to the big, modern cities: Beijing, Shanghai, Guangzhou. In the countryside things are different, with old attitudes still prevalent. I heard a story recently about a young peasant girl who was kissed on the forehead by a young man, and was then expected to marry him. When she did not, she was subjected to so much obloquy that she killed herself.

But you will probably be going to the cities, so watch out for a roller-coaster ride in social attitudes. Every year when I visit China and talk to my Chinese colleagues and friends, I see change. The revolution continues.

Western businessmen of all ages will meet lots of young women. Many of these are keen to get a 'ticket out of China', either through marriage or by finding a sugar-daddy to subsidise their planned college course in the United States. Others may be looking for work. Some may have no hidden agenda at all, other than liking the look of you (but I am cynical enough to think the latter are among China's smaller minorities). Relax. Encounters with these ladies are always pleasant; they are polite and will not force themselves on you if you do not want to go beyond a chat.

'Hostesses', who hang out in hotels and certain bars, are a lot less discreet. The rules are that you have to buy them drinks, at exorbitant prices. Anything more, and you have to get negotiating (see Myth 8, though negotiations are usually rather faster than those with a SOE).

True love can also spring up across cultures. There is now a much greater acceptance of mixed couples, which is quite remarkable when we consider that even six or seven years ago attitudes to this were still very conservative. (During the Qing dynasty (1644–1911), intermarriage between a Manchu and a Chinese was strictly forbidden, and until the late 1970s it was forbidden for a Chinese to marry a foreigner.) You may still encounter some stares and possibly abuse (to your partner), especially outside the cities, but the problem is much less than it used to be. Remember that there are stupid and ill-natured people in every country.

Myth 5

Guanxi is a time-consuming sideshow to the real business of business

MYTH

We all need contacts, especially to get things moving. But they are not at the heart of business, which is about long-term value – recognising it, providing it. This is a universal truth, which over time the market will enforce, as 'cronyist' businesses fail to keep up with modern ones that use objective criteria of value.

Right now, China is rapidly developing a legal structure and a more professionalised business cadre. More Chinese are being educated abroad and/or being exposed to Western ways of doing business. *Guanxi* will become seen more and more as an anachronism and a hindrance to proper, Western-style business.

REALITY

The Chinese do not measure things by money, so the market cannot shout down the old values. Money matters, of course, but the truly successful person is influential and well connected. Wealth is simply one means to that end.

Guanxi, or 'relationships', consists of connections defined by reciprocity, trust and mutual obligation; in other words, friendship with implications of a continual exchange of favours. Etymologically, *guan* is a derivative word meaning 'door' or 'pass', while *xi* is a very old word with connotations of 'hierarchy' (a point I owe to Tim Ambler of London Business School). Therefore, the term literally means 'door into a hierarchy or group'. You are either on the right side of the door or the wrong side of it!

The notion is very much influenced by the Confucian values of 'face' and 'social harmony': all three are inter-related. If you conduct an honest and sincere relationship and respect a person's place in the hierarchy, you increase social harmony. If you reciprocate obligations and keep your promises, you preserve face.

People in China still have little confidence or trust in the legal/regulatory system and prefer to trust their personal relationships. There is a different attitude in Western countries, where one can do business with people one does not know well or whom one even dislikes, and get the legal system to back you when disputes arise. *Guanxi* assumes some of the functions of a legal system – 'mutual favours' were not traditionally viewed as corruption – and is a code of conduct substituting for the rule of law.

Rushing into business before you have established relationships is a recipe for disaster. *Guanxi* is still fundamental to business success in China: you must have a solid network of business and government contacts.

Guanxi is a catalyst or lubricant to get things done in China by opening doors to resources. It circumvents or neutralises the bureaucratic system. With the right *guanxi*, there are few rules in China that

---

The king of *guanxi*

Hong Kong businessman Vincent Lo is sometimes known as the 'king of *guanxi*'. He spent many years courting the Shanghai government, and participated in many key government events. Perhaps his most notable success was the redevelopment of a piece of real estate in Shanghai in the decayed Xintiandi district. He restored it to its 1930s look and today Xintiandi is a major restaurant/bar/shopping centre and part of the standard tourist route. When the central government announced recently that it would focus economic development in the Western regions of China (its 'Go West' strategy), Vincent bought a series of dilapidated cement plants in Chongqing. He promised no lay-offs, stuck to his promise, and today is cashing in on an infrastructure boom.

He is quoted as saying that the ingredient for success was persistence and understanding the culture. 'Americans always bring in teams of lawyers,' he says. 'They will be stuck there forever.'

can't be broken or at least bent: I have heard *guanxi* described as 'a tool to achieve the impossible'.

There are numerous examples to illustrate the intelligent development and use of *guanxi* by foreign companies. A classic story is that of General Motors. Although Ford had entered the Chinese markets years ahead of them, it was GM who ended up leading the market. Their CEO John F. Smith developed extensive relationships with many Chinese officials at different levels, as well as hiring Shirley Young, the daughter of a prominent Chinese war hero, to create relationships and educate them about Chinese culture. This won GM the first bid to produce cars in China. (They were, it must be admitted, also helped by the fact that China's much-loved former premier Zhou Enlai had a Buick. Maybe if Ford had been able to persuade Chairman Mao to drive round in one of their cars ...)

AIG, the giant American insurance company, took the long view when dealing with China. CEO Hank Greenberg spent 17 years courting central and provincial officials. In 1992 AIG was the first foreign insurer permitted to sell insurance policies. Greenberg was asked why AIG got the rights and was reputed to have said 'What have you been doing for the last 17 years?'

He understood that *guanxi* must be mutually beneficial: 'If the relationship is being built just to benefit the foreigner, you might as well stay home.'

One of the top four foreign joint venture consultancies has recently employed the daughter of a very senior Party member to 'open doors'. This is a wise move, and nobody in China will think anything different.

A personal example of *guanxi* at work: a colleague of mine was in trouble. His work visa was due to expire in three days time and to go through the normal channels would have taken at least four weeks (he would have to have reapplied as if he were starting the whole process from the beginning, and would have been in breach of the law until the new visa arrived). Using a *guanxi* connection with a friend who knew someone from the Public Security Bureau, which issued the visas, my colleague was able to obtain a renewal in one day.

Guanxi is different from the Western concept of networking: it is long-term and concentrated, whereas networking is about having a wide range of acquaintances. A second difference is that in the West a business relationship has a group implication, whereas, in *guanxi* the ties are always personal. Personal loyalty is more important than loyalty to the organisation. This is an essential point I will expand later, as a lot of Western companies fail to understand the implications of this fact. Finally, *guanxi* has to be seen as part of a 'holistic' ethos, embracing all the roles in Chinese life.

Introductions are a huge part of *guanxi*. Westerners often ask Chinese for introductions without understanding what this involves. If I introduce you to people in my *guanxi* network, that places an obligation on them to put themselves out for you. In return, I will have to do them a favour later.

Note that favours will probably be unequal to start with. You, a newcomer, have little to offer the important dealmaker who sets things up for you. But the system is long-term. The expectation is that *over time* you will repay him or her with favours.

How do you attain guanxi?

Guanxi exists in four forms, based on relationship closeness. These are as follows (in descending order of importance):

- *Jiaren*. Consists of family members. Chinese families are more extended than Western ones (though the one-child policy will have a dramatic effect on this); consider, for example, the huge family around which the classic saga *Hong Lou Meng* (The Dream of Red Mansions) revolves. Non-family can be co-opted into this network, but it is rare. I have about 80 people in this network.

- *Zijiren*. A small group of really close friends. They say 'you can count your true friends on the fingers of one hand': these are very special people with whom no favour is too much.

- *Shuren*. These are more distant friends or colleagues. Usually there is some long-standing or formal tie. *Shuren* often come from the same village or area (this means much more to Chinese than to Westerners) or are fellow members of societies (the Chinese love forming and joining societies, especially from school and college days). You will have a lot of links in common.

- *Shengren*. These are outsiders, who look as if they might be useful contacts (or good friends) but about whom this judgement has not yet been made. Such a judgement can take a long time, as Westerners eager to get to China and 'get on with stuff' soon find out. The first three categories are unlikely (for most Chinese) to include Westerners: this category may well include some. As you get older, you tend to have fewer *shengren guanxi*: either you know and trust people (and they are in the 'top three' categories), or they are just acquaintances.

There are a number of ways in which foreigners improve their chances of acquiring *shuren guanxi*:

- A Chinese husband or wife. You are now caught up in the net of family obligations that is Chinese society. There are now people who can be shamed if you do not deliver on a promise.

- You speak perfect Chinese. This does seem to elevate foreigners to the position of 'honorary Chinese' even though you still have the ability to leave China and never come back. Perfect Chinese implies you have committed time and effort to the study of China and its ways, as well as meaning you can participate in conversations at all levels. Da Shan, who is actually a white Canadian who presents language programmes on CCTV (China Central Television, China's BBC), is a model example of this.

- You are a 'friend of China'. Henry Kissinger is still used extensively by foreign companies to open doors in China. Kissinger was, of course, instrumental in opening up China to the West in 1972: the Chinese remember such gestures and retain long-term bonds with such people. Clearly we cannot all be Henry Kissinger, but there are smaller-scale benefits foreigners can bring to China which will be valued by your local hosts.

It still looks hard for an ordinary Western business person to qualify for the necessary *guanxi*. I make three comments.

First, it is essential for your business to have *guanxi*, otherwise it will fail. If you cannot acquire it yourself, you need an intermediary. Note that even if you follow this route, you must understand the *guanxi* system and how it works.

Second, foreigners can develop what I call 'probational *guanxi*' quite quickly. As I said above, the very fact of your bringing a business to China implies you are at least beginning to fall into the 'friend of China' category, and the longer you stay in China (and the more resources you are seen to be committing to it), the stronger this will become. In practice, you will begin to form alliances the moment you start doing business, and these are best treated as if you are developing formal *guanxi* – which may end up happening. Hence my term 'probational *guanxi*'.

When you arrive, and are seen to be of some importance, you will be invited to enter individuals' networks. The Chinese work very hard to cultivate new friends: most foreigners in China are targeted quite hard, as they are perceived to be well connected and wealthy. Is this cynicism on behalf of the Chinese? By idealistic standards of, say, a Western romantic novelist, the answer must be yes. But be more subtle: a wise view is to admit that the Chinese have a strong vein of pragmatism in how they form and maintain relationships, but at the same time people can and do form friendships. Bear in mind the phrase *duo yige guanxi, duo yitiao lu*: 'one more connection offers one more road to take'. (There is also a 'flip' side to this quote: *duo yige diren, duo yizhou shan*: 'one more enemy creates one more mountain'.)

In practice, Chinese people place foreigners in three categories. Working upwards, we begin with people with whom we have no real plan to form a relationship. A tourist visiting China would be an example of this, or a journalist who takes a very anti-Chinese view of things. Second are people with whom it is expedient to build a relationship, but who are not respected. Examples of this category would be the classic expatriate manager who spends all his or her time in a special foreigners' compound, moaning about China and counting the days till his or her next placement. Such a person needs to be dealt with, but will only receive superficial politeness. The third category is the foreigner who is both perceived as important politically (in the broadest sense of the word) and respected.

To place oneself in this third category should be the aim of everybody coming to China to do serious business. And such a person will find themselves making real steps onto the *guanxi* ladder.

Finally, the more you are perceived as thinking like a Chinese person, the more quickly you will be welcomed into real *guanxi* networks. An American friend of mine managed to succeed in doing this immediately when he landed in China. When he invited Chinese out to a restaurant, he would get involved in the ritual haggling, explaining, exactly as a Chinese would, that if they didn't let him pay, that meant they were looking down on him. Let people know that you understand the rules of the game, and that you intend to stick to them, and you will be invited to play.

When guanxi goes wrong

One of the persistent issues for foreign companies is who owns the *guanxi* relationship. The foreign company employs a Chinese person to form the *guanxi* because he/she has the connections, speaks the language and intimately understands the culture. Because the person is employed by the company, Westerners assume their company owns the relationship. Yet the reality is that *guanxi* transactions are always personally based. It is a one-to-one relationship. If employees leave the company they will take their *guanxi* with them, not hand it down to their replacements.

If this is not well managed, abuses can occur. In one example I know, the sales representatives of a beverage company obtained favourable credits for the distributor at the company's expense. This action not only enhanced the sales manager's connections, but was also a way of paying back favours from the past. It bought no benefit to the company at all, but was part of a larger process in which the company was just a means to personal ends.

China commentator Wilfred Vanhonacker cites the example of a Chinese sales representative of a Western pharmaceutical company, who also sold drugs on the side from a Chinese company. He suggests that there are some ways forward for front line personnel such as the following:

- Open the procurement process to competitive bidding. Currently, procurement is probably done via the *guanxi* network, which probably suits your procurement officer fine, but may not mean your company is getting the best deal.

- Develop a team-based approach. Many foreign companies are now moving to team-based selling and thus creating multiple points of contact, rather than the previous system whereby customer contact revolved around a particular individual. A team-based system can work well in some sectors, but may have drawbacks, especially when dealing with the government ministries where the *guanxi* culture is still dominant.

- Develop loyalty-building activities in the company with your 'frontline' Chinese employees. Examples might be allowing employees to bring their families to visit the company, or engaging with employees outside office hours in activities like visiting the fitness centre together. More radically, allow frontline staff to be managed by close friends of the management team or founder of the company. These activities have already been implemented by some companies in China.

- Rotate sales and procurement people regularly. To me, however, this is 'cutting off your nose to spite your face'. Connections are the essence of these functions. Find better ways of managing than this.

It is important for managers not to get paranoid about this. Salespeople in the West have been known to take clients with them when they leave! Sensible management procedures should ensure that the right balance is struck between personal and company interest.

What you must not do with *guanxi* is suddenly change the rules. Crocodile was a major Singaporean retail outlet, mainly for sportswear. Since the early 1990s, Crocodile and its JV partner, Shanghainese Fan Juanfen, had seen its textile retail business grow twelvefold. Fan Juanfen was a classmate of former Vice-Premier Li Lanqing, a very powerful figure in the government. Crocodile used Fan's *guanxi* to get around the then-existing laws prohibiting foreigners from owning retail outlets. They set up trading companies and took minority shares in the stores; the trading companies and the stores shared common warehouses and the goods simply moved from one side to another. The rift began when Crocodile sent a manager to oversee the operation in preparation for a stock market listing. Fan's role was questioned; rows began; in 1998, Crocodile fired Fan.

A few months later she registered another company called Captaino, took over the 19 previously Crocodile stores (and all the employees) and started selling the remaining merchandise – the store leases were, after all, in her name. Crocodile responded by accusing

Fan and 18 employees (including her sister-in-law, brother-in-law, sister, brother and a niece) of siphoning off money to buy private flats.

The legal battle is still raging. Between them, Crocodile and Captaino have spent 15 million yuan in legal fees.

How did Crocodile get into this mess? They forgot the value Fan had put into the company through her *guanxi*. On top of that, by firing her, they made her lose face. From a Chinese perspective, Fan saw it as perfectly correct to share wealth with her relatives, and felt insulted by her dismissal.

Note that this was a Singaporean company making this mistake, not a Western one!

Finally, do not assume that developing *guanxi* guarantees success. McDonnell Douglas entered China in the 1970s, taking time to cultivate *guanxi* with Avic, the Chinese state aerospace group. In 1991, they signed a $6 billion deal in 1991 to build over 150 planes in China. However the client airline (CAAC) was under the control of another ministry, whose officials were courted by Boeing and Airbus and sent on 'cultural visits' to the United States (a very useful negotiating ploy). The end result was that McDonnell Douglas built only two planes in China. The deal was finally cancelled in 1997.

CONCLUSION

Guanxi is essential to doing business in China. Without relationships, you are taking a leap in the dark, or as the Chinese say, 'turning up at the temple door without a pig's head' (the traditional symbolic gift to heaven).

Take time and effort to accumulate your network, and do not delegate this task. Always return favours – failure to do this results in 'loss of face' all round and undoes any good work you have put into the relationship. *Guanxi* should be treated as a major part of your company's strategy and not just an incidental accessory.

At the same time, the relevance of *guanxi* does vary. It is most important in dealing with government and SOEs. When dealing with joint ventures and private companies, things vary. Some companies are more objective about business benefits than others. But I have yet to encounter a business in China where contacts are not important. And certainly, if you venture outside Beijing or Shanghai, *guanxi* has universal power.

Manage your *guanxi* like your bank account. After so many favours (credits), you will need to pay back (debits), even if it is not a convenient time to do so, in order to continue meet your obligations in the relationship and thus to retain face. The Chinese have turned this art into a carefully calculated science.

Guanxi has been translated as different things by different translators. Network? Connections? Relationship? Probably the most useful word is 'trust'.

While I stress the importance of *guanxi* here, and elsewhere, don't forget that it is a necessary but not sufficient condition for success in consumer markets. Ultimately products succeed or fail the world over because they fill a real market need (or fail to do so). No amount of *guanxi* will persuade people to buy products that are no use to them.

The Chinese are irrationally xenophobic

MYTH

Chinese people don't really like foreigners however polite they may be on the surface. The old view of '*yang guizi!*' (foreign devils!) remains in the psyche. You can't do anything about this – just put up with it.

REALITY

There is some truth to this: some Chinese do think that way, especially those who are less educated and who have had less contact with foreigners (though of course it is not that simple – nothing in China is). But note that some expatriates are very good at fuelling prejudice by arrogance, rudeness and inappropriate behaviour.

All Chinese people are justifiably proud of their long history and civilisation and the survival of their rich culture over the last three millennia (see box at the end of this chapter). At the same, the Chinese remember the imperialist humiliations of the nineteenth century.

These began when the East India Company started to pay for Chinese tea and silk with opium instead of silver. (The Victorian stereotype of the sinister oriental opium den conveniently overlooked the fact that Britain had sold the sinister orientals the opium in the first place.) Addiction rose sharply, and things reached a crisis point in the 1830s when the level of demand became so high that China began to pay for the opium not just with tea and silk but with the reserves of silver they had been paid for their products in the first place. In 1840 the emperor forbade the trade and ordered the destruction and confiscation of opium chests. This led to the first of the opium wars, which China lost, unable to match the firepower of

British gunboats. China was forced to sign the humiliating Treaty of Nanjing, whereby it paid huge indemnities, ceded Hong Kong and opened new ports to foreign trade.

This was just the beginning of a long series of foreign interventions, with the main Western powers getting involved in a kind of 'scramble for China' to match their 'scramble for Africa'. This resulted in more gunboats, and a series of concessions under successive humiliating treaties. Subsequent events such as the Sino-Japanese war (1937–45), the Korean war (1951–3), the border dispute with the former Soviet Union (1961) and the Vietnam conflict (1964–72) all served to increase Chinese distrust.

This historical sense is deeply embedded in the Chinese psyche. For example, during the US–China trade talks in 2003, China's Vice-Premier Wu Yi was confronted with a deluge of complaints that the Chinese government was not cracking down hard enough on Chinese companies selling counterfeit products. She is reputed to have countered that many of the cultural relics in US museums were plundered from China.

The Communist era regularly churned out crude anti-foreign propaganda. Before 1976, for example, it was common to see references to foreigners as 'foreign devils' or 'barbarians' in school textbooks, and to the peoples of Hong Kong and Taiwan as 'traitors' who wanted to see China controlled by Western capitalists. The generation who studied these books are now in their fifties, and some of what they read has inevitably has rubbed off onto their consciousness.

Many people perceive a real 'threat' to China from the outside world in the form of Western values, and there is a sense in which they are right to see this. My own position is that this threat is actually proving quite weak at the most basic levels, and that the opportunities of change are much greater, but I can understand people, especially in the older generation, who do not see this.

One of the main problems is a simple lack of contact with Westerners due to China's isolationism in the past. On a recent trip to the Forbidden City in Beijing, I went with a group of Caucasians and found myself and my colleagues being stared at by Chinese visitors, especially ones from outside the capital. On another occasion, when friends of mine from Norway visited me in China a couple of years back, we went to a small town called Huairou. Whilst walking in the town centre, scores of children came up to us and stared in amazement at my two blond, blue-eyed friends. Some started to touch their hair. My friends experienced no threat: they knew this was simple curiosity, from people who had never seen anyone remotely like this before. Huairou, incidentally, is only 35 miles north of Beijing.

Visitors who venture deep into the countryside can encounter genuine hostility – but again this is not always the case. Chris has many tales of great kindness and friendliness on his rural expeditions in *Journey to the Middle Kingdom*. And remember that unpleasant encounters can happen anywhere in the world, for example to a Chinese venturing into rural areas of the 'civilised' West.

Chinese attitudes to fellow Chinese working for foreign companies can be bizarre. Foreigners are often treated as 'guests' in China; their Chinese employees can have a much harder time. When I worked for a Western company in China, I had many more problems with the company security guards than any Westerner. On a number of occasions I entered the building with one of my Western colleagues, and was asked by the security guard to show my pass, while my colleague was waved through. I felt angry at this, and asked my Chinese colleagues how they felt about it. In a typically Chinese pragmatic way they said it was necessary to show it for security reasons, as a lot of theft was going on. Most of the thefts were being carried out by locals and therefore it was not surprising that all Chinese had to be stopped.

In general, I would say that Western Caucasians have a relatively 'easy ride' in China when it comes to everyday matters. Regrettably, I have also seen Westerners abuse this hospitality, which of course reinforces stereotypes and encourages xenophobic behaviour. 'China bashing' still seems to be a pastime in some of the expatriate bars and compounds in China by ignorant and uninformed foreigners.

Other visitors to China can experience difficulties.

Overseas Chinese (huaqiao) form a powerful economic bloc outside China and dominate the economies of many of the countries they live in, particularly in south-east Asian countries. The Chinese diaspora numbers around 60 million and can make good partners with Western businesses. Much of the foreign direct investment in China comes from overseas Chinese, partly driven by the rational, economic lure of low wages, partly thanks to ties of blood and kinship.

However, there are differences between mainland Chinese and their overseas counterparts. Yes, there is a strong sense that all are 'part of the Chinese family', but many mainlanders have ambivalent attitudes and feelings towards their wealthier overseas counterparts. There is some degree of envy here, and some puzzlement as to why their overseas counterparts are more successful when they have nothing special about them. (Conversely, the overseas Chinese wonder why the mainlanders are not as successful, and wonder if they are stupid.)

Some *huaqiao* make themselves unpopular with mainlanders by flaunting their wealth or other displays of arrogance. Anecdotal evidence suggests that many overseas Chinese from Hong Kong have incurred hostility by their arrogant behaviour towards locals. Taiwanese are perceived to be well mannered, rich and to have excellent Chinese, but are also seen as complicated, indirect in communication, and, beneath their exteriors, distrustful of local Chinese.

Some overseas Chinese do not understand modern China, expecting it to be a kind of theme park where 50 years of communism never happened and everything is traditional and quaint.

Overseas Chinese are jokingly referred to as 'bananas' because externally they are ethnically Chinese, but internally are considered to have a 'Western' mindset. (On the other hand, Caucasians who are very culturally sensitive and understand China well are amicably called 'boiled eggs': white outside and yellow inside, they think and act like the Chinese.)

When using overseas Chinese in China as managers or intermediaries, you and they need to be fully aware of these complex issues.

The Japanese still face prejudice as a result of the appalling behaviour of their armies in the Second World War. The Rape of Nanjing, where hundreds of thousands of citizens were murdered by the invading Imperial forces, is only one example. Japanese firms seeking to do business in China must be aware of this historical background.

I know Chinese colleagues and friends who share a strong sense of discomfort when working with Japanese people due to past events. This is unfortunate, given that one would like to move on, but it is a fact of life. Both my grandmother-in-law and my mother-in-law remember the horrors of the war when they were young women, and never forget to tell me of it. One vivid memory they retain is seeing young girls under fourteen being dragged away from their homes to be used as sex slaves for the Japanese Army.

A couple of years back, the Chinese government protested to the Japanese government about the way the brutal treatment of the Chinese was airbrushed out of Japanese history books. There still has been no public apology as such from the Japanese government.

Japanese firms have also acquired a reputation for discriminating against Chinese employees. I do not know if there is truth behind this, but if you are a Japanese reader, please be aware of this, and do not fan the flames of rumour.

Africans can still find themselves on the receiving end of prejudice. There is no historical reason for this as far as I can see, but sadly the prejudice is often worse than that faced by Westerners or Japanese. During Mao's reign, there were contacts with African nations as part of China's aid to Third World countries, and images of Africa and Africans used to be displayed in publications. But actual contact was limited; much of this prejudice is still due to ignorance.

Actually, Caucasians face the least innate prejudice: the most common Chinese reaction is a mixture of respect, fear and above all puzzlement. The basic Chinese view is that foreigners are coming to China to make money, but in the process are also helping the country to modernise. This is a fundamentally fair deal, and is accepted. There are also some who perceive Westerners as technologically advanced but morally corrupt.

The Chinese attitude to expatriates depends at least partially on the expatriates themselves. Those who are well qualified and culturally sensitive are highly respected. Sadly, many expatriates make themselves unpopular with the Chinese. Some companies have made the mistake of sending people of average calibre and of no outstanding technical expertise to China, presumably to keep them out of head office. Unfortunately, this type of foreigner behaves with the arrogance of a Manchu emperor, taking a disdainful attitude to ordinary Chinese. 'Everything Western is best', is their motto. Chinese get fed up with their constant 'China bashing', endless criticisms of China's old ways, hygienic standards, inefficient ways of working, and so on and on. Americans, I am sad to say, are often the worst offenders here.

Young Chinese, in particular, are annoyed by 'China bashing'. Older people often put up with it, believing that the West is somehow perfect. Younger Chinese know otherwise, and have more confidence in their own country. Once you know a Chinese person well, you can share a joke about the hassles of life in Beijing, but it is best to let them introduce the subject first.

China bashers are usually blissfully unaware of what the Chinese think and feel about them. The Chinese attitude to this type of person is total disrespect – internally. They do not show this, however, until some real test of loyalty is posed.

The salary differential between expatriates and Chinese is an added cause for resentment if the expatriate is less well qualified than the local (or perceived to be of low calibre).

Take, for example, the case of a local Chinese manager who was ready and prepared to take on a more senior role in a multinational joint venture company. But he was not promoted to that position. Instead, an expatriate was brought in, who may have had international experience but lacked any local knowledge or understanding of Chinese customs and practices. The new appointee was also younger than the bypassed Chinese manager.

The Chinese perception of this was that it was just another example of foreigners trying to subjugate the Chinese people, albeit in a modern setting and without actually using gunboats or imported opium. Nothing was actually said, but feelings were strong and the manager was demotivated. This demotivation soon spread to other Chinese managers and workers in the organisation.

Another factor contributing to the Chinese stereotype of foreigners is that the majority of expatriates living in China wall themselves up in compounds, just as the old imperialists did (a sign in the main park in the 1920s Shanghai 'concessions' read 'No dogs or Chinese allowed'). I am glad to say that this is gradually changing, with a new and younger breed of expatriates in China who tend to live in high-rise buildings and share them with the Chinese new rich.

It is an open secret that many overseas managers take – and flaunt – a local mistress. In many cases the mistress will be given a job with the company as part of her 'reward'. She may even then get quick promotion to higher positions in the company. This type of behaviour is abhorrent to the local Chinese. To be fair, there is a double standard here, as if a local Chinese manager took a mistress (which is common), he would be less frowned on.

CONCLUSION

I do not want to end this section on a negative note. Generally, the attitude of the Chinese to foreigners is a combination of respect with some distrust and distance. They do not hate or fear foreign people. They are wary of their influence, however, given China's bitter experience with the outside world. The foreigner going to China is highly unlikely to face any hostile reaction, but rather to be treated with humility, hospitality and politeness. This is as true – or maybe even more true – for women as for men.

Many Chinese, especially the younger generation, do not feel any prejudice, and of those who still do, most can be won over by fair dealing, respectfulness, politeness, understanding – and time.

China: the world's oldest surviving culture

The Chinese are justifiably proud of their cultural history. No other nation on earth can boast such a long and uninterrupted story, and for much of that time the 'Middle Kingdom' was the most advanced society on earth.

If a Martian had done a tour of the world in, say, 1420, he/she (it?) would have been in no doubt which was the most civilised nation on earth. Massive Chinese junks under the command of Admiral Zheng He had visited India, Arabia and Africa. The new Ming dynasty was flourishing. China's cities were vast, and its system of government infinitely more sophisticated than in the warring city states that made up most of Europe. Chinese art and technology were similarly miles ahead.

Chinese culture can trace its roots back to the Shang dynasty, which flourished around 1500 BC (there was an earlier dynasty, the Xia, but little is known of them apart from some Chinese myths such as the story of the Yellow Emperor and the invention of agriculture by Shen Nong). Artefacts that survive from the Shang period include 'oracle bones', which were used for divination (the Chinese were as superstitious then as now). Characters would be written on these bones, which would then be heated. Fate would decide how the bones would split in the heat and the characters which survived this process would foretell the future. The great thing about these 3,500-year-old characters is that they are recognisable antecedents of the writing in use in China today. We also know that the Shang were an agricultural people, with a strong priestly caste and the practice of ancestor worship, who made fine bronzes. It is revealing to compare this legacy with the sparse Western knowledge about the people who built Stonehenge.

The Shang were replaced by the Zhou (the Chinese cyclical notion of time is rooted in the rise and fall of dynasties: they begin as vibrant and reforming, and slowly become conservative, obsessed with their own power and decadent). The high point of the Zhou was around 1000 BC. Later, this dynasty too degenerated. The work of Confucius springs from this period: the Sage of Qufu looked back at the 'golden age' of the early Zhou and modelled social and political practice on how things were then. Much of modern China, still Confucian at its heart, is thus actually modelled on a society that existed 3,000 years ago. Before mocking this, Westerners should consider the value of such a rootedness in time.

Confucius' words were ignored in his day, however, and the Zhou empire collapsed into a ragbag of warring states. During this violent era, Sun Zi wrote his great *Art of War*. Finally, in 221 BC, a strongman arose from this anarchy, the great unifier of China (from whom the country gets its Western name), Qin Shihuang. Mao expressly modelled himself on this ruthless but effective man, once commenting (at the height of the Cultural Revolution), that Qin had only buried 860 scholars but he intended to bury 86,000. People in China were expected to understand this reference. The British Prime Minister making some comment about a third-century BC tribal leader might not get such a response.

Dynasties rose and fell. Qin's own fell very quickly, as he was so loathed, leaving only his terracotta army in Xian, and was followed by the Han, the Sui, the Tang, the Song and the Yuan (to name the major ones before 1368). The Han gave their name to Chinese ethnicity. The Tang are regarded by many as the high point of Chinese civilisation: Xian was the greatest city in the world in the eighth century. Buddhism became a part of Chinese culture at that time, thanks to the opening of the 'silk road' to the West. The Song saw a flourishing of art and philosophy. The Yuan were the Mongol rulers visited by Marco Polo 500 years later.

In 1368 the Ming dynasty came to power – in the usual style, by means of a rebellion against a decadent central power. This intensely conservative dynasty ruled China for nearly 300 years, during which time it was finally overtaken by the West in terms of technology and society. Many Chinese believe that this overtaking has been merely a blip – if one assumes it began around 1500, it still makes up only 14 per cent of the time since the Shang rulers founded their kingdom – and assume it is only a matter of time before China regains its natural position as the most powerful and successful nation on earth.

In 1644 the Ming were replaced by invading northerners from Manchuria: the Qing dynasty. This drove many Chinese to underground resistance; many legends of martial monks come from this era, as do the original Triads. In fact, however, the invaders took on all the ritual and values of the Ming, modelling themselves totally on traditional Chinese models. Like its predecessors, this dynasty in time became decadent. The West did not help by flooding China with opium and invading it, but China also produced its own internal squabbling in the form of the Taiping rebellion, an extraordinary uprising led by a man who believed he was the brother of Jesus Christ. The rebellion is reputed to have cost the lives of 20,000,000 people.

The old dynasty was finally dragged down by its own conservatism and corruption; all attempts at modernisation were stymied by the Dowager Empress Ci Xi. In 1911, China became a republic.

Despite the idealism of its founder, Sun Yat Sen (or Sun Zhongshan – most Chinese cities have a 'Zhongshan Street', and the traditional 'Mao suit' should properly be called a Zhongshan suit) the republic did not last. Sun died, the squabbles began.

Mao was the son of a peasant (as the first Ming emperor had been) who went to the city to study. By the 1930s he was a leader of the Communist Party – and surrounded by republican troops intent on wiping the Communists out. The Long March, which he instigated, was an extraordinary escape from encirclement, covering thousands of miles of the worst terrain imaginable. The march is a matter of great pride to Chinese (especially the older generation). The nearest parallel we in the West can imagine as a nation-forming piece of mythology are the trenches of the First World War or (for the more optimistic) Dunkirk.

Mao actually came to power in 1949, making his famous speech from the top of Tiananmen Gate where he proclaimed 'the Chinese people have stood up'. Mao was, in essence, a Stalinist ruler (a huge picture of the Soviet dictator used to adorn the Avenue of Eternal Peace (Chang'an Dajie) in Beijing). Economic reform only began slowly after his death in 1976, but took off in 1985 with the rise to power of Deng Xiaoping.

The mask of Fu Manchu: the myth of inscrutability

MYTH

The Inscrutable Oriental is an old myth. Modern managers, eager to dispense with such creaky old stereotypes, enter China with open minds ...

... And after a few years of muddle, misunderstanding, apparent dishonesty (etc., etc.) come to the sad conclusion that this is not a myth but a reality. You just can't make these guys out!

REALITY

The Chinese are not 'inscrutable' – to fellow Chinese. They have few problems 'reading' one another. Instead, they often find Westerners hard to understand, distrusting their apparent openness and wondering what is really going on beneath all that flashy bonhomie. Table 7.1 summarises some of the key different attitudes between Western and Chinese peoples.

Westerners should understand the literary and philosophical traditions behind how and why the Chinese communicate. Young Chinese are taught at home and at school the story of the *Three Kingdoms*, one of the four classic novels in Chinese literature. The story is set at the chaotic end of the Han dynasty, and is full of strategy and political intrigue in the Emperor's palace. One of the rulers of the Three Kingdoms was Liu Bei, and he has become a role model for many Chinese on how they should conduct their communications in public.

Liu was a general who aspired to be a king, but was defeated in battle and had to flee. He found sanctuary at the court of Cao

Table 7.1 *Key differences in attitudes of Westerners and Chinese*

Chinese view of Westerners	Westerners' view of the Chinese
– too direct and can give offence	– unwilling to express open disagreement
– use colloquial, unfamiliar language	– opinions are not expressed strongly
– dominate in meetings (which shows that they don't think the Chinese are competent)	– don't want to share information
	– difficult to tell if silence and nodding mean 'Yes' or 'No'
– difficult to tell if they are serious or joking	– don't show physical signs of urgency or excitement
– tend to be culturally arrogant	
– expect a quick, simplistic response to complex questions	

Cao, who was the prime minister of one of the strongest states. Here Liu hid his thoughts and emotions, adopting a low profile and living an ordinary life, like someone with no ambitions. One evening he was invited by Cao Cao to a banquet and during dinner the minister announced that he and Liu Bei were not ordinary people but heroes of the kingdom. On hearing this, Liu feared that his secret ambition had been revealed, but he was saved by a violent thunderstorm that broke at that moment. He hid under the table to show how frightened he was (and to disguise his true strength and ambition).

Later on, Cao Cao asked Liu Bei to lead his army against some invaders, which Liu victoriously did. After this, he set up his own kingdom, using some of his host's soldiers and horses.

The moral is, of course, that if Liu Bei had revealed or expressed his fears and ambitions to Cao Cao, he would not have acquired his own kingdom. Like him, we are not supposed to express openly our emotions or any personal intentions, thoughts and desires.

The idea is also expressed strongly in the classic Daoist text the *Dao de Jing*: 'He who knows, speaks not; he who speaks, knows not.'

My grandfather used to say that 90 per cent of people's problems come from the mouth. If we eat too much we get sick; if we speak too much we unconsciously give away our business, family and personal secrets, which will then be used against us.

Educated Chinese will know the saying of Confucius *qiang da chu tou niao*: 'the gun always shoots the first bird in a flock'. Showing off is regarded as very poor behaviour in China.

Just before my school examinations I was reminded by my parents not to boast about how hard I worked to pass them. This would constitute showing off; it would create envy and make those who were not successful feel even worse, especially if it were said in front of them. My parents were extremely tough on this, as are the parents of most Chinese children.

At work, if a Chinese person gets a promoted, it is very rare for them to celebrate via a big party or an evening out with champagne. Any celebrations will be quiet and among close friends.

The hierarchical nature of Chinese tradition is especially strong in SOEs, and you will find it in joint ventures and private companies too. One aspect of this is that leaders often expect their subordinates to 'sense' how they should communicate with them. They may get used to this, and expect the same from you.

There are some implicit rules governing communication patterns in the work environment such as:

- Junior staff display deferential attitudes to senior members of staff to indicate their 'respect' and the belief that there is a 'right way' to do things.

- People should avoid open confrontation and conflict (save 'face' all round).

- Behaviour is generally characterised by *low assertiveness* and a *high degree of co-operation* to foster social harmony.

Breakdowns in communications can be serious and long lasting. When harmony is disrupted between two people because of a conflict in the workplace, the parties will be very unwilling to confront each other directly to discuss and sort out the issues. Instead, each person will expect the other party to 'sense' the problem and to hint a little that they are aware of this. This means that finding a resolution can be a very slow process. The experience is known in Chinese as the 'knot that ties the heart' (*Xinjie*) It is important not to offend a Chinese host, because the impact could last a long time.

This has happened with me in China: the friendship is virtually over, although this has been unsaid. If there is to be a solution, it will have to come by a third party intervention, from friends or family.

The power of friendship

Friendship in China is hugely important. I know it matters in the West, too, but there is an added dimension to Chinese friendship. In Chinese culture, friendship is taken very seriously: people will go to the end of the earth to help a friend, and even face death! Between really 'true friends' – the phrase sounds slightly stilted in the context of Western culture, where people are used to talking about 'true love', but it fits Chinese culture perfectly – there are unlikely to be any communication problems or blockages. It is to their true friends that Chinese people tell all their secrets. There is a Chinese saying: *zhi dui peng you cai neng tao xin wo* (Dig deep down into your heart and show it to your true friend).

A friendship from the past is still used as a model in modern China today. Bao Shu Ya and Guan Zhong were very close friends from childhood days. In adult life, they used to do business with each other. Guan often took more than his fair share of profits, but Bao did not mind as Guan was poor and had to look after his old mother.

Later on, both men applied for official positions, the route to success in traditional China. Guan secured a position serving a certain Prince Jiu, while Bao served a Prince Xiaobo. Unfortunately, these two princes ended up fighting for the throne. Prince Jiu was killed and Guan was imprisoned. Bao recommended to Prince Xiaobo that he should not only release Guan but appoint him as the new prime minister. The Prince agreed and Guan was appointed to the position, which was higher than that of Bao's. Guan proved excellent at the job: after seven years, the State of Qi became the strongest state in China. Guan often said that although his parents bore him, it was only Bao who really knew him. In modern China, the phrase 'friendship of Guan and Bao' is used to describe two people who have a truly good friendship and shared mutual understanding.

Classic Chinese literature makes much of friendship. *The Water Margin* is all about what we would now call 'male bonding', and the *Dream of Red Mansions* about the interplay of friendship and love.

The two main characters in the *Dream of Red Mansions* are the cousins Jia Baoyu and Lin Daiyu. Baoyu, a boy, rebelled against traditional customs, refusing to read the conventional books that he was supposed to read. This annoyed his father so much that he was made to copy articles from these books 100 times. Lin Daiyu, a girl who loved Baoyu, helped him copy the articles, even though she was extremely ill with lung problems inherited as a child. The tragedy of the story is that Daiyu was not able to express her love openly for Baoyu, because this was not the done thing at that time. Given the Chinese style of 'high context' communication, he was supposed to sense it. He did, finally, but his parents had other marriage plans for him … I shan't give away the ending.

The novel demonstrates powerfully the true nature of deep friendship and personal sacrifice. It shows, better than any management book ever could, why the Chinese attach so much importance to friendship and the sacrifices that one needs to undertake to show the depth of commitment.

These issues are hugely important in my life: my true friends are those with whom I can feel free to ask any favour, from putting me up to borrowing money (as they, of course, can ask the same of me). I find that in the West, lending money to friends is not common. If done, it is done reluctantly. My parents used to drum into me that really true friendship should know no bounds.

Chinese culture and context

At a deeper level, every language comes with a different parcel of assumptions, references, expectations – a parcel usefully referred to as subtext. The problem that arises from the existence of subtext is self-reference. We look at the surface of what is communicated and unconsciously attach our own subtexts (cultural and personal) to it, rather than the ones intended by the speaker. Dealing with new cultures, we have to learn to become aware of these 'hidden differences'.

A further difficulty comes from the fact that some cultures use more subtext than others. This is captured in the concept of 'high versus low context'. In *high-context cultures*, such as China, communication depends on the context or non-verbal aspect of communication, i.e. interpreting what is meant rather than what is actually spoken and has the following characteristics:

- What is unsaid but understood carries more weight than the verbal or written contract.

- Social trust needs to precede agreement.

- Agreements are made on the basis of general trust.

- Negotiations are slow and ritualistic.

- Relationships and goodwill are highly valued.

In *low-context cultures* such as Germany and Switzerland, communication depends more on explicit, verbally expressed communications and has the following characteristics:

- Interpretation depends on what is actually said or written.

- Expertise and performance are valued above reputation or connections.

- Legal contracts are necessary and binding.

- Relationships are not a priority.

- Negotiations are expected to be quick and efficient. Why waste time?

Figure 7.1 illustrates the continuum for the different cultures of the world between high and low context communication patterns. The continuum illustrates the potential disaster scenarios that may occur. People in high context cultures (such as China) expect others to understand and to decode gestures and unarticulated moods and tones. A person from a low context country (the United Kingdom,

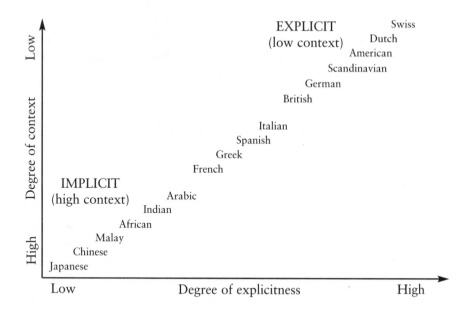

Figure 7.1 *High and low context communications*

Source: Hall and Hall, *Understanding Cultural Differences*

United States, Germany, Switzerland, etc) would perceive Chinese behaviour as mysterious and even perhaps underhand, because high context communicators do not reveal too much verbally.

The 'high context' approach to communication is to set the context first. Thus the Chinese will present all the factors of a situation, the background, any side issues and so on, and only then give their own personal views or recommendations. It needs to be emphasised that this sequence of 'Because … therefore …' is the normal structure of everyday Chinese communications.

In the first ('because') stage, the context will be set up. This will include praise for various people involved in whatever it has taken to get things to the point they are now at (even if such people will play no role in the proceedings!). It will also cover current issues. The objective of the speaker is to ensure that all points of view are taken into account, and hopefully in the process minimise any obvious disagreements and ensure that no one will lose face or is being treated unfairly or aggressively.

In the second ('therefore') stage of the communications sequence, recommendations are made. The Chinese speaker will still stress mutual benefits and strive for some uniform approach; if things have been done badly in the past, they will hint at this by saying things like 'We need improvements in the area of ...', rather than come out with outright criticism.

In contrast, many Western nations have a low context culture, which means that their sequence of communications is diametrically opposite. They are more likely to fire in the recommendations first, then follow up with the reason. This clearly implies 'getting on the job or task'.

I have observed many interactions between Westerners and Chinese. Foreigners can become very impatient with the 'because ... therefore ...' approach – an impatience that sometimes explodes into outright arrogance. I remember being in a room with a group of Western business people listening to a speech by a Chinese speaker, and the audience began to groan and comment out loud that the speech was irrelevant and not getting to the point. In fact, they were missing some key points of the 'context' of the message. To be fair, the Chinese speaker was being particularly long winded, but the guests would have done better to have listened politely.

Ultimately this all boils down to a fundamental difference of approach: for the Chinese, business communication is about building relationships, while in the West it is about efficient exchange of information and getting things done as quickly as possible (and if a few feathers get ruffled in the process, well, that's business).

Many Western personnel in China seem not to understand this. I have a friend who works for a joint venture company in Shanghai. Her general manager is a German who has had extensive international experience. However, he has created great ill feeling in my friend (and other Chinese managers) by repeatedly telling them what to do. The Chinese felt insulted; they were being treated as if they lacked intelligence and understanding. In fact, the German manager did begin to think they were stupid, because they did not give him the direct feedback he expected: instead, information was conveyed the Chinese way, informally, indirectly. A vicious circle of misunderstanding and disrespect grew and grew. At the time of writing, it is still growing, with damaging consequences for morale and the business as a whole.

Chinese notions of space and time

Chinese notions of space and time are very different from Western ones. Personal space, as one would expect in a country of 1.3 billion people, is much smaller than Westerners are used to. Chinese tend to stand very close to each other, and while waiting in line will jostle one another, which can drive a Westerner insane, especially one who is used to waiting in an orderly fashion.

Try shopping in Nanjing Road in Shanghai or getting on a Beijing bus at rush hour to test this assertion.

Chinese perception of time has always been more cyclical than that of Westerners. For the Chinese, with a long history of dynasties rising and falling, recurrence is a real and meaningful theme. In contrast, Western, Newtonian time flows in one direction.

This has implications when it comes to business meetings in China. In general, when it comes to dealing with joint venture companies, the appointment times are as in the West. When meeting government or SOE officials, however, you should arrive on time, but will probably have to wait for the Chinese side to arrive. Expect this, and do not get upset, even if it is irritating. Outside the business context, time schedules tend not to be adhered to: guests arriving for a dinner invitation can arrive an hour late or even an hour early (they will help you cook the meal!).

Westerners tend to measure out time equally, to maximise efficiency. Time is perceived as a limited resource that needs to be used effectively; hence the phrase 'time is money'. Chinese time echoes the Buddhist tradition, which teaches that time is flexible and qualitative: a moment spent contemplating a beautiful scene is of more value than many dull hours. This idea is exemplified in the *guanxi* situation: when you drink wine with a true friend, a thousand glasses are not enough; when you drink with a person that you cannot get on with, one glass is too much.

Furthermore, if there is a linear, regular aspect to Chinese perception of time; it has a much slower pulse. My father used to say: 'What is one year in a man's life?'

CONCLUSION

It all goes back to understanding the culture. If you understand the culture, you will be able to decode signals better. As you and your Chinese counterparts work together, you will be able to form a bond with them, as a result of which they will start revealing their true thoughts about things (though in private, not in public). Over time, this friendship can become very real, and communication can become very deep.

At the same time, never forget that behind their apparently cold exteriors, the Chinese are very sensitive. If you alienate someone, be prepared to take an indirect route to patch things up. The following guidelines will be useful:

- Start by understanding the Chinese view that relationship building is key to breaking down communications barriers.

- Wear formal suits to meetings. Women should look smart but not too sexy.

- In the initial stages of meeting the Chinese, formality rules. Address the leader first (and keep talking to the leader throughout if you are dealing with an old-fashioned company). Always address people by their titles when dealing with SOEs or government: in joint ventures you can be more informal and call the Director 'Mr Wei'. Do not use given names (remember that the given name comes second in China: Mao Zedong's brother was Mao Zetan). Note that Mr Wei's 25-year-old son and daughter will probably have given themselves a Western name, which they will want you to use – once they have said you can. Such informality does not suit the older generation, but their children are at ease with it.

- Frankness in communications in China is almost always considered rude. Better to be subtle.

- If you ask a question in a meeting and get either no answer or an oblique response, do not push the point. It has something to do with face and it is better to approach the person in a private context.

- Avoid expressing criticism of an individual in front of others. Respect the importance of face and honour to the Chinese.

- The Chinese are more comfortable with silence in communications than Westerners. It is considered to be a virtue. It is also (often) a signal that you should carry on talking. Silence from the

Chinese is also a form of communication and, just as important to understand, the meaning will depend on the context. Giving a presentation, if you ask a question and are greeted by silence it may mean people do not understand, or that they are not sure what answer you want to hear. Best to rephrase the question, and if you still get silence, move on. In meetings, if a senior manager is present, junior staff will not speak.

- The Chinese are much more reserved when it comes to expressing emotions than their Western counterparts. This is consistent with the Confucian tradition of preserving face and balance. This apparent lack of emotion – which is, of course, lack of *expressed* emotion – is probably the main reason for the myth of Chinese 'inscrutability'.

- When a Chinese person laughs, it is likely they are hiding embarrassment or discomfort. So please do not take offence: it is a defensive posture, a way to save face.

- Chinese make less eye contact than Westerners. This is a matter of degree: you should still make eye contact when you address people. But avoid staring! The crowds that stare at foreigners are, by formal standards, being rude, though I think it is fairer to say that they are overcome by curiosity.

- Physical contact should be restricted to handshakes: American-style backslapping does not go down well.

Fu Who ...?

Fu Manchu was the Oriental villain of a series of books written in the 1920s by British author Sax Rohmer. They are full of adventure and action – and ethnic stereotyping of the worst kind! Fu himself is sinister, cruel, cold-hearted (etc.) and of course inscrutable. Rather than get upset about the racism that flows through them, the books are now best regarded as a joke. Like all the best jokes, there is an element of truth behind them: not, of course, in the nature of the Chinese, but in how the Chinese can be misunderstood by the West.

Rules are rules: negotiating in China is like negotiating everywhere else

MYTH

Negotiation is about objective benefits. If you get subjective, you lose. At the same time, there are rules: for example, a deal is a deal. There may be people who duck and dive, renege on contracts and behave unethically in the name of ancient culture, but over time the market will find them out and isolate them.

REALITY

Maybe this view will prevail in the long term, but for now you have to negotiate with China as it is, and the rules are very different!

This is especially true when dealing with government or SOEs, but even when dealing with multinational joint ventures or private companies it is important to understand the traditional Chinese approach to negotiating, however Western things may at first seem.

The Chinese are certainly amongst the toughest negotiators in the world; they have learned this from childhood, bargaining in shops, or at market stalls. Bargaining comes as naturally to many Chinese as brushing their teeth. You will notice that the Chinese negotiators often seem obsessed with minutiae of price. Reason? China is still an agrarian society. The street market is still in many people's minds, and behind this, folk memories of eking out a living, where every 'fen' saved was important.

This is not surprising given that over 800 million Chinese still live in the countryside. Many of China's best and brightest originate from the rural sector and then find positions in the major SOEs or joint venture companies (a time-honoured tradition: in the imperial days they would have entered the civil service exams, then left their village to take up a position in the governing bureaucracy). Such people retain strong roots in a rural culture, based on group cohesiveness and harmony rather than the individualistic values of Western societies or of China's new, post-Deng generation.

The second cultural strand that affects the negotiation process is Confucianism: respect for hierarchical relationships, preservation of face and group harmony.

Fused with Confucian values are Daoist notions of searching for 'the way' (*dao*) and balance between extremes (Yin and Yang). The first of these means that Chinese negotiators will be more focused on means than ends, on process rather than goals. The correct way of proceeding may have priority over objectivity.

A further cultural strand influencing the Chinese negotiating style is the Chinese attitude to foreigners (see Myth 6), which can involve a measure of distrust and wariness.

Many Western business people arrive in China with a one-page list of etiquette – how to eat stir-fried scorpions or drink eel soup and similar handy tips – tons of business cards, an army of interpreters and so on. This certainly gets them through the revolving door, but not far enough for a sustained and prolonged relationship. The Western negotiator needs to understand the broader context of Chinese culture and values. Educated Chinese have studied from childhood two classic Chinese texts, *The Art of War* by Sun Zi and *The 36 Strategies*. For Western negotiators to enter China without some knowledge of these two books is like walking into a battlefield without ammunition.

Two classics
The Art of War (*Bing Fa*) by Sun Zi was written over 2,000 years ago. It is considered the most comprehensive book on military strategy ever written, not only in China but in Japan and Korea.

Although the exact details of Sun Zi's life are sketchy, it is reputed that he lived at about the same time as Confucius and was appointed a general in the Kingdom of Wu, winning many battles for the kingdom over the course of thirty years. His *Art of War* is the most influential text in classical Chinese strategic thinking. It was also required reading in management and business strategy programmes during Japan's economic development in the 1960s and 1970s.

It should be required reading for anyone seeking to do business in China now, as well. (There are numerous editions: the quotes below come from translations by S. B. Griffith and by T. Cleary, both of which are available in paperback.) *The Art of War* is wide-ranging, covering issues from the key principles of strategy to the role of training, from the qualities that make a superior general to the use of secret agents.

What are its main messages?

The most important is probably the importance of outwitting your opponent. Not just via surprise – though this is a key aspect of Sun Zi's philosophy – but by subtly *manipulating* the enemy to do what you need them to do in order to put them at the maximum disadvantage.

One key to achieving this is the acquisition of information: the best-informed side usually wins. Understanding the personal weakness of the enemy general is a key. If he is impetuous, offer him the chance to do something rash (and disastrous); if he is cowardly, attack; if he is obsessed with honour, insult him; if he is compassionate, wage a war of attrition (and so on).

Numbers alone have little value. Intelligent generals 'use the strength of their enemies to defeat them' – a notion taken to heart by Mao Zedong, whose guerrilla army defeated the numerically and technologically superior Japanese and Kuomintang by using classic Sun Zi tactics.

The other key to manipulation is deceit. The more you can fool the enemy about your character, numbers, strengths, intentions and so on, the further ahead you are of them in the mental battle that is strategy. You should fool the enemy into thinking you are being manipulated by them, but actually you are in charge. You should perpetually change your methods and plans 'making it impossible for others to anticipate your purpose'.

'All warfare is based on deception,' Sun writes. 'Therefore, when able to attack, we must pretend to be unable; when employing our forces, we must seem inactive; when we are near, we must make the enemy believe we are far away; when far away, we must make him believe we are near.'

What does not appear anywhere in *The Art of War* is any notion of

'fairness' or rules of engagement. It is assumed that there are none –
and there certainly were none in the time when Sun Zi wrote. General
Sherman's comment, that 'war is hell' was as true in Master Sun's day
as it was in the American Civil War.

(Note: another missing aspect is technology, which is not discussed.
Sun Zi assumes that all participants have access to similar technology,
which no doubt they did in Warring States era China.)

The 36 Strategies was complied after the time of Sun Zi – it uses
some of his ideas – but not long after. Nobody knows who the author
was. The strategies are grouped under six main categories, three for
attack and three for defence. There are six strategies in each category
(naturally: Chinese love neat groups of numbers).

- *Advantageous strategies* are for use when you have a numerical or
  other advantage, and are largely about making best use of this,
  not overextending your forces or frittering advantage away.

- *Opportunistic strategies* are self-explanatory. For example
  Strategy 12, 'Stealing a goat along the way', reminds the reader
  not to miss opportunities, however small.

- *Offensive strategies* are about decisive actions. Note that none of
  these advocate massed, frontal attack. Maybe General Haig
  should have been sent a copy in 1916.

- With *confusion strategies* we enter the world of defence, or at
  least of overcoming apparent disadvantage. Create confusion in
  the enemy.

- *Deception strategies* are self-explanatory. One example is Strategy
  27, 'Pretending to be insane but staying smart.' Contemporary
  Chinese negotiators may not feign insanity, but they can often
  'play dumb', especially if they feel they are being patronised by
  Westerners.

- Finally, there are *desperate strategies*. Wisely, the last of these is
  'Escape: the best scheme'.

China: a nation of strategists

The Chinese always think strategically. If they appear to be avoiding specifics and remaining general, this is not an attempt to avoid the issues but a natural consequence of their approach. As mentioned above, strategy books such as *The Art of War* and *The 36 Strategies* are standard reading for educated people.

Chinese stories often involve clever strategic ploys. Here is one I learnt as a boy. The story dates, as many such stories do, from the Warring States era (476–221 BC). This was a time of perpetual conflict. It was the golden age of classical Chinese strategy – though it was probably not much fun to live in unless you were a general.

General Tian of the Kingdom of Chi would race horses with the princes of Chi as a hobby. The usual procedure was to have three races and the traditional approach of the General was to pit his best, middle and worst horses against similar horses of the princes. One day, however, General Tian approached his master strategist for advice, and the strategist recommended that he should race his worst horse against the prince's best, pit his best horse against his rival's middle one, and then use his middle horse to compete against his rival's worst. This advice was followed, the General won two races and lost one, and was declared the overall winner of the contest.

In the twenty-first century – the Warring Multinationals era? – this model is being used by Haier in the white goods sector. They have entered the US market and adopted a strategy of selling their best range of products against the medium-range American fridges, and have quickly gained a decent market share.

Both these classics have a strong influence of Daoism. They can sound quite mystical – 'be as unfathomable as the clouds, move like a thunderbolt', advises Sun Zi – but there is nothing mystical about the consequences of ignoring these classics.

One of the first rules in negotiating in China is that signing on the dotted line is only the beginning of your negotiations, not the end of it as envisaged by many Western companies. Be prepared to revisit your contractual obligations, detail by detail.

Another rule is not to underestimate the Chinese. Many Western firms do this; I've seen it happen time after time. The Chinese may not look sophisticated or slick when compared to their Armani-suited Western counterparts. But let me assure you they know your company and Western practices much better than you know China and its ways of doing things.

In most aspects of Chinese life, there is a public and private level of operations. Negotiations are no exception. The public face of negotiation is what takes place in conference rooms and boardrooms, with many people involved in the process. It is this type of negotiation that is protracted and requires infinite patience. It is during such negotiations that both parties try to understand what the other party or means. The contract is *part* of this aspect of negotiation.

The private face of negotiations involves discussions outside the confines of formal conference room settings. Generally, the Chinese do not appear to be direct about their objectives in formal negotiations. Sometimes negotiations can stall at this stage, and that is when you need to meet one or two members of the Chinese team on a personal level outside the formal arena.

The critical success factors here are the ability to sing karaoke songs and to smoke, and the amount of drink one can handle! I am not aware of this being on any MBA syllabus (except, perhaps, the drinking), but maybe there is an opportunity for an entrepreneurially minded business school here. It is in these situations, when the Chinese are relaxed, that they will open up more and reveal what is really on their mind. This process will also cement any personal relationships you might have developed with individuals. As you may have noticed, I believe that personal relationships are the critical element in business relationships in China.

I was involved in a lengthy negotiation with a joint venture company to deliver some senior management training. The negotiations were protracted, even by Chinese standards: cumbersome, laden with excruciating details of the programme and consistent demands for guarantees of quality. This was, of course, a tactic to wear me out so I would give in to concessions. At the same time, I was informed that they were talking to my competitors about the same programme (this is normal in China: please do not feel upset or angry when this happens). So I invited the two key negotiators for an excellent, enjoyable (and expensive) dinner. There we broke the ice, and we signed the agreement the next day.

The moral of the story is to move away from the public level of negotiations: as an old Chinese saying goes, 'sometimes it is better not to take the straight road to your destination'. The specific nature of the diversion from the straight road is important too: food. The Chinese, as you will know, love food. This is not about guzzling, but the whole ritual associated with eating. Sharing and enjoying food with people has enormous symbolic importance in China.

Note that you may have to eat, drink and be merry with quite a few people. Different people in the organisation will have their own agendas. In dealing with government, you probably need to make friends at both national and local level. So get in the party mood and enjoy the process! A core skill, as in selling and negotiating anywhere, is to determine who are the influencers and decision makers at each level. Your intermediary should be able to help you here.

Chinese society is still very hierarchical and there is great respect for authority, so Western companies sending in people to negotiate can be sure that the Chinese will take a keen interest in the authority and status of those at the negotiating table. Sending someone with high status will be perceived by the Chinese as showing respect to them as well as demonstrating that the negotiations are being taken seriously. If the Western firm send someone of insufficient rank, this will be construed as a loss of face on the Chinese side. This can be turned to advantage: send in senior lead negotiators, which will be seen an honour (the right initial strategy); send in junior people if you feel you are being messed about.

Guanxi are at the heart of negotiation. Chinese participants will want, and probably expect, a level of personal relationship with their counterpart in the negotiation that Westerners would consider unnecessary and even undesirable. This expectation can be seen by some in the West as a cynical plot to create an emotional bond and thus a more favourable attitude towards the Chinese side. This is unfair. From a Western perspective personal friendship may be derived from a business relationship: the Chinese prefer things the other way round. Establish relationships as a basis for business deals; build ties that extend beyond the negotiation table.

Another cultural feature of Chinese life is the tremendous respect for social etiquette and ritual. Traditional hierarchies were maintained through ritual and rites. Even today, ritual is part and parcel of social interaction. Expect a high level of formality in the negotiating room.

The traditional values of patience and persistence, plus the bureaucratic mindset inherited from the communist system, result in the infamously protracted Chinese negotiation process that can take months or even years to complete. This is often perceived by Westerners as a Chinese ploy to extract further concessions. Sometimes, as in my story above, it is – but usually it is an unconscious, cultural bias. I have experienced this process many a time and have had to adjust my expectations to match the Chinese perception of time. Yes, things are changing, especially now many Chinese managers are being educated overseas. But this will depend on whom you are dealing with and which business sector is involved. If you are negotiating with SOEs, it is more than likely you will be involved in a very long negotiation process. With private enterprises and joint venture companies, the process should be quicker.

The negotiation process
In this section, I shall use the model of Paul Kirkbride, Sara Tang and Robert Westwood, who broke the negotiation process into four stages.

- *Exploration* is where the parties assess each other's position and flexibility, examining the character, background and personalities of those involved.

- *Expectation structuring* is where the parties 'spin' the available information, trying to create unfavourable perceptions of their opponents' position and favourable ones of their own. It is also at this stage that each party will attempt to condition the other into an expectation of concessions and compromise.

- *Solution building* is where the focus changes to making concessions, 'horse-trading' and moving from the initial positions to search for a mutual basis for agreement.

- *Finalising* involves reaching an agreed outcome, hopefully with a win–win scenario.

Applying this model to China ...

The *exploration* stage is a lengthy process. There are two reasons. The first is that the primary focus for Chinese negotiators at this stage is to determine how much *guanxi* they have in the situation and how much they can hope to gain from the interaction. Time must be spent on the *guanxi* process. The second is that the Chinese will at the same time be establishing overarching principles and exploring general areas of mutual benefit.

For Westerners, this phase is sometimes dismissed as ritualistic and non-substantive. This is a mistake. It is during this phase that the Chinese 'holistic' perspectives are established.

The Chinese also avoid detailed discussions at this early stage because they want to avoid potential conflict. This will be a dominant theme throughout the negotiations, even later on, when substantive issues have to be dealt with. Chinese negotiators prefer a low-key approach and adopt avoidance strategies when it comes to conflict.

The Chinese dislike of conflict can seem hypocritical to Westerners: 'they want to nail us to the floor and do so without any argument'. Once again, the Chinese cultural starting point has to be understood to make sense of this. Conflict is perceived by the Chinese as a zero-sum game with 'winners' and 'losers', with the latter losing face in the process, which is to be avoided at all costs. In an extreme case, the Chinese will discontinue a meeting or withdraw from the negotiations altogether simply to avoid conflict.

There are, of course, occasions when Chinese can be very aggressive and rude. This is uncommon, but I have heard of foreign businessmen who have experienced the sharp tongue of a Chinese negotiator, sometimes with a xenophobic comment such as 'you only come here to exploit us', 'you don't speak our language' or 'what do you know of China?' If this happens to you, do not get drawn into a slanging match. The negotiator has lost face and you now have an advantage over him. You have probably touched a raw nerve somewhere. Can you think where? He may have just revealed a major strategic flaw. He may now be looking for a quick exit, in which case you may allow him one if, and only if, it suits you. If it does not – well, he is the one who broke the rules and the onus is on him to restore the situation.

Attempts to speed things up via aggression or appeals to emotion (tactics I have seen Westerners use on Chinese) will backfire seriously here, only making the Chinese more cautious and reserved. There is a saying in Chinese: 'harmony makes you a fortune'.

Western negotiators should avoid a confrontational style, but should set high initial demands. The Chinese will; do not be shocked by this. The aim is to have room for manoeuvre later, when the aim of the bargaining process is to reach for, and to be seen to be reaching for, compromise solutions.

Note that there is a strong sense of collectivism on the Chinese side: Westerners need to appeal to the *group* rather than to an individual member of the negotiating team. You may deal with individuals later, 'off-line', but when in the negotiating room, you and they are parts of two teams.

During the second, *expectation structuring* stage, the Chinese will probably heap praise on you, which may be construed by Westerners as unnecessary flattery or humility. (The converse *may* occur: the Chinese may attempt to use 'shaming' tactics. This works well inside Chinese society, where it is one of the most powerful mechanisms of social control, but most Chinese realise it will not work with foreigners.)

Chinese negotiators will always deny any critical comment about their company or organisation, even if they are well aware of the shortcoming. This is because they will not admit failings in front of their colleagues, or in front of a foreigner. This can be a problem, especially in a sales situation, when you are looking for buying signals such as 'we need more X' or 'we've a problem with Y'. The way round this, of course, is to build relationships with individuals. In a one-to-one context; once you have established personal relationships with particular people, they are more likely to tell you the true story.

The third, *solution building* phase reflects the Chinese holistic perspective, which involves seeing things in wholes rather than in parts. This stems from Daoist philosophy, which emphasises the relativity and inter-relationship of everything, and perhaps explains the strange (to the West) Chinese negotiation process, where nothing is settled in stages but matters are resolved in one great swoop at the end. The Chinese can suddenly come out with a compromise solution without having gone through any explicit verbal horse-trading.

Compromise has different meanings to Westerners and Chinese negotiators. From the Western perspective, compromise implies give and take, trade-offs and mutual concessions, and to some degree is seen as a sub-optimal solution. For the Chinese, compromise is a natural, healthy outcome. Mutual benefit and commonality of purpose have been achieved. The Chinese will downplay the fact that both sides have retreated and highlight that *both sides have finally recognised their mutual interests*. A compromise is a reconciliation of mutual interest and therefore an optimal solution. Harmony has been achieved! If you have actually won major concessions in the deal, you should not advertise the fact.

At the *finalising the agreement* phase, there is a fundamental difference in perception and attitude. For the Chinese, formalisation of a contract does not imply that it is final and fixed. Numerous cases exist of Chinese companies trying to renegotiate agreements after they have been signed.

For Westerners, this is the apotheosis of bad faith, the final proof that the Chinese are devious, untrustworthy, conniving (etc.). But for the Chinese, formalisation of agreements simply meant that the parties really do understand each other, and therefore there is now a real platform for further horse trading and mutual exchange of favours. This view is, of course, derived from the Chinese perception that business is about the continuous development of personal relationships: our old friend *guanxi*.

Chinese businessmen trained in the West are abandoning some of these precepts, although their approach will vary depending on whom they are negotiating with (if they are negotiating with SOEs, they will revert to the traditional Chinese format of negotiations). But my view is that you should always assume traditional procedures will be followed, unless you know the Chinese team to be very Western-minded and they explicitly state that they have a preference for Western-style negotiation.

CONCLUSION

Table 8.1 summarises the key differences between Western and Chinese perceptions and procedures in the negotiation process. Understand these, and use the understanding to your advantage.

Remember that at the end of the day, Chinese negotiators, like their Western counterparts, do want the final goals and ends. Be patient.

Table 8.1 *Different perceptions and negotiation procedures*

	Chinese	Western
Negotiation focuses on:	Process	Content
	Means	End
	Generalities	Specifics
The outcome is:	Trust	A legal contract
A contract is:	A summary of discussion	The point of it all
	A 'snapshot of the relationship'	
	Mutable	Binding
Fairness is assessed by:	Procedure	Outcomes

Adapted from Ming-Jer Chen, *Inside Chinese Business*

Chinese business people are not trustworthy

MYTH

'You can't trust the Chinese. They'll steal intellectual property, welsh on negotiated deals and many of them are corrupt.'

REALITY

Business in China is harsh, and operates by different rules to those in the West. The key to retaining one's judgement in China is to understand the rules, and thus learn the difference between someone who is fundamentally honest but playing by different rules from you, and someone who is an out-and-out crook, with whom local people would have no truck.

There will of course be crooks, for obvious reasons. One is simply numbers: there are a lot of Chinese and a proportion will be 'rotten apples'. China is also emerging from the shadows of socialism, where commercial activities were all frowned upon: business ethics are a new topic for many people. Add the fact that there is little transparency or regulatory enforcement – and also the traditional Chinese determination to get rich – and you cannot expect perfection! Remember that the problem is not exclusive to China: look at the former Eastern European and Russian economies. Of course, I do not condone such people, and the purpose of this chapter is to help you spot and get round them. There are plenty of honest (by local standards) business people out there.

Finally, do not fall into the trap that I have seen some foreign companies fall into, of using ethics as a kind of all-purpose explanation for cultural misunderstandings. 'Those devious ***s cheated us' may feel better than 'We failed because we didn't understand the culture', but it doesn't lead to learning or good business.

There is an expression in Chinese, *shang chang ru zhan chang*: the marketplace is a battlefield. Bear this in mind. As we have seen, Chinese military strategy is based on deception, so expect deception in business too. Westerners often perceive this as 'dishonesty'. Such a judgement is dangerous.

Let us look more closely at the three areas outlined in the myth.

Intellectual property rights (IPR)

It is no secret that China is currently the world's largest producer of counterfeit products, infringing patents, copyright and trademarks to produce all sorts of things from designer clothes to computer software. The Chinese government's own Development Research Council estimates that counterfeiting in China is a $17 billion industry.

From a Western perspective, such actions cannot be condoned. However, the phenomenon needs to be examined more closely.

Why is piracy so extensive in China? The Software Publishers' Association carried out surveys in different countries asking whether people thought it right to use software without paying for it. The majority of respondents in countries such as Italy agreed that this was wrong, but in countries with strong Confucian traditions the practice was seen as less unethical. Confucian culture puts stress on individuals sharing what they create with the group and society. Infringements of IPR are not seen as theft in the way that stealing someone's purse would be.

A traditional story tells of a very poor boy in imperial times – when there was no state education and all lessons had to be paid for – who had to leave school because his parents ran out of money. This boy secretly went to the school and hid himself under the windowsill to listen to the teachers. Eventually he passed the imperial examination with flying colours and achieved official rank in the government. The boy has always been portrayed as heroic, overcoming barriers to study. The fact that he technically 'stole' intellectual property is irrelevant.

In addition, many Chinese are lukewarm about Western attitudes towards intellectual property rights, seeing them as an attempt by developed countries to monopolise technically advanced products.

Some of the Chinese people I know do not really see what all the fuss is about, and these people are college and university graduates. There is a genuine sense that IP is really no big deal.

Behind this lies a long historical precedent of 'laws made to be broken'. China has had 4,000 years of authoritarian rule. For centuries the Chinese had laws imposed on them by different emperors, some benevolent and others brutal. This gave rise to a mentality whereby Chinese people uphold the rules publicly but flout them when they have to (and when they believe they can get away with it). It is a survival strategy. Hence there is a tendency not to feel guilty about ignoring or circumventing the system. A large proportion of Chinese behaviour can be described as driven by expediency, by the need to get by in an often harsh world.

This propensity to break 'rules' is partly conditioned by Confucian philosophy, which values the 'rule of man' over the 'rule of law'. Hence the Chinese are more likely to follow the wishes of a very powerful figure, as shown, for example, by the enormous cult following of Chairman Mao, whose actions in instigating the Cultural Revolution in 1966 exemplify the power of one individual over rules and regulations.

Some commentators do not accept the argument that China's culture creates a different attitude to IPR than is found elsewhere. It is a matter of political will, not culture, they say. This attitude displays their ignorance and arrogance. IPR violations occur in the first place because of cultural attitudes formed from thousands of years of subverting the system in China.

At the same time, IP theft is not just a Chinese but a global problem. IPR violations occur all over the globe, from the former eastern European nations to Indonesia, Taiwan and Singapore. For example, Kroll Associates in Hong Kong uncovered a global operation in consumer goods pirating: a Chinese factory was used for the production, but the operation was financed from Taiwan, the goods were shipped to India then on to Panama through a trading company registered in Hong Kong to a final destination in Brazil. The Chinese counterfeiters were actually just doing the spadework: the real criminal brains, and the real profits, were elsewhere.

And of course, faking goods happens in the West, too. I recall a factory in Reading, England, for example, that was raided and closed down for producing fake Chanel perfumes.

The good news for foreign companies is that IP protection is improving in China. China has written and rewritten hundreds of IPR laws and enforcement procedures to implement one of the most important WTO agreements, the Trade-Related Aspects of Intellectual Property Rights Agreement.

The problem is enforcement, which is not yet up to international standards. One cannot expect this to happen overnight. Foreign companies should bear in mind that China's compliance is a long-term target: to expect full, immediate compliance is a tall order, because the process involves an extensive transformation. Enforcement difficulties stem from a number of factors:

- The complexity of the regulations causes difficulties and delays.

- China does not have a unified, integrated force for IP rights: there are many different bodies involved.

- The sheer size of China complicates the implementation of all legislation.

- There is a shortage of highly trained people.

- There is corruption in the Chinese judicial system.

- There is inadequate education about IPR to the general public.

- Enforcement is sometimes 'blocked' by provincial government officials, because whole villages are involved in the production of pirated products. Closing them down would lead to massive unemployment and political tensions.

What can foreign companies do about IPR violations in China?

As mentioned above, various IP bodies are monitoring the situation and are making progress. IPR consciousness is rising in China, due in part to court cases, access to the Internet and the Chinese media's coverage of violations. It is acknowledged that what is needed in China is education to instil respect for intellectual property and this is happening, albeit slowly.

The Chinese government has a vested interest in taming the IPR

Right or wrong?

It could be argued that there are two possible responses to IPR viola-tions in China. One is based on cultural relativism, which argues that one country's ethics are no better that any other's, leading to the conclusion that there are no international rights and wrongs. The opposite to relativism is cultural imperialism, which argues that what is right within a firm's home context is right for whatever country they operate in.

A 'middle way' involves making judgements on a case-by-case basis. That is tougher to do, but in my view a much better approach.

---

violations beast: in the future, China will want to protect its own domestic technology companies.

Currently, it appears that the multinational companies are resigned to the fact that China will take time to get its act together. Right now, they are adopting a range of tactics to protect their IPR. Measures include:

- Raising awareness among your staff that IPR violations are not acceptable.

- Encouraging the reporting of IPR theft. A film company in Beijing recently set up a reward for anyone who reported counterfeit copies of the company's movies.

- 'Making poachers into gamekeepers'. Cadence Design Systems, a large, US-based supplier of electronic design automation, has managed to get the Chinese companies who pirated its products to become licence holding companies – who now have an interest in stopping the IP from spreading any further.

- Conducting due diligence on Chinese partners. Horror stories abound of multinationals finding that their partners are setting up factories down the road to compete against them, using their IP. Keep a constant eye on stakeholders, and integrate your operations if possible.

- Protecting your IP by registering your product in China. Many companies do not do this, however, as sensitive IP has been known to leak out of the patent department. I advise following their example, and simply seeking to beat the competition by out-executing them – but your lawyer will no doubt advise otherwise.

- Talking to other companies in the same sector. This could help you share your problems and perhaps combine forces to deter potential piracy.

I have observed a gradual crackdown on IPR violations at street level. Three years ago, you would constantly be approached in the street, restaurants and bars by hawkers peddling counterfeit CDs and DVDs. In 2004, this activity has been reduced substantially. Yes, it still happens, but not on the scale of the previous years. How much this represents the true scale of crackdown overall is debatable, but nevertheless, something is stirring.

High-tech investment in China

Western high-tech multinationals, including many Fortune 500 companies such as Microsoft, Intel and IBM, are already setting up sophisticated and high-level research centres in China. These companies clearly believe it is worth the risk of losing IP to invest in China.

Why are they doing this? China has an enormous talent pool. Its universities produce thousands of engineers and programmers each year. These are high-quality graduates: most students entering the top Chinese universities have to pass extremely difficult entrance examinations. China has just under 3 million university students, selected from a population size of 1.3 billion; the United States has around 17 million university students from a population of 290 million.

A high proportion of Chinese graduates are scientists: the pragmatic streak in Chinese culture has always valued science over the liberal arts, so other disciplines like languages or law were not considered serious subjects. Science graduates tended to get more jobs in the past. (Confucius, a liberal arts man to his boots, has been ignored on this

---

issue!) Even though this has started to change, with business-related subjects becoming popular, mathematics and science are still studied up to a very high level until just before university entrance. Many Chinese students who sit the American GMAT examinations do exceptionally well in spite of their relatively poor English: they excel in the mathematics section. GMAT scores of 700 or more are not uncommon, while the global average is around 600.

The investing companies also want to use China as a model for other developing markets. Alcatel, the French telecom company, has set up a large research centre in Shanghai with many Chinese engineers working on advanced projects. One project involves looking at how Chinese mobile phones switch from one network to another, so that they can improve the switching process for the next generation of mobiles for the entire world market. Alcatel reason, quite correctly, that IP theft is not just a Chinese phenomenon; it will be encountered in all emerging markets. China is as good a place as any to learn how to handle it.

A third argument is used by some biotechnology companies working in areas such as stem cell research. Here, China is leading cutting edge research because it does not have the barriers faced in the West, where companies are confronted by ethical and moral dilemmas. Visitors to Chinese markets will have noticed that animal rights do not figure very highly on the Chinese political agenda (though this may change – ask my partner!)

Negotiation practices

One of the commonest complaints against the Chinese is that they chop and change their minds after a deal is signed. This is true, and should be understood and worked with rather than railed against. Remember that in China, signing on the dotted line is only the beginning of your real negotiations, not the end of it as envisaged by many Western companies. If foreign businesses understand this, they will have made a strategic leap in their thinking about the China market.

Note that the 'renegotiating' Chinese are very unlikely to renege on their contract; they are simply continuing to jostle for advantage. It is all part of the 'war of the marketplace'. Remember that Sun Zi has nothing to say about 'fair' or 'unfair': war and negotiation are about who has the upper hand, the best bargaining position at any given time. Sorry, but that's how it is.

The other classic Chinese strategy text is *The 36 Strategies*, alluded to earlier. I've already given an outline of the book: here I will look at a couple of strategies in depth.

Strategy 4, one of the aggressive strategies, is 'Conserving energy while the enemy tires himself out'. This will be used when there is no urgency to rush the deal and when time and resources are to your advantage. You have no need to make a direct attack: sit and watch your adversaries as they blunder round. Try to lead them up as many blind alleys as possible, a bit like a tennis player putting the ball in alternate far corners of the court. The final strike can then be quick and simple. There are many historical examples to illustrate this strategy (in the West, it was used by the Roman general Fabius to vanquish the previously unbeatable Hannibal).

As Wee Chou Hou and Lan Luh Luh point out in their excellent translation of the classic, this strategy was employed by Japanese companies in the 1960s and 1970s, when they embarked on their global penetration of Western markets. At the time they were weak in comparison to the Western giants, so could not take them head on. Instead they stood back and chose their moment to compete in markets or segments where competitors were weak or there was no competition. Japanese car companies did not launch a frontal attack on Ford and GM, but built capabilities and experience in what seemed quiet, 'backwater' segments. Japanese cars became well known for quality, reliability and high fuel efficiency. American gas-guzzlers despised their neat, compact Japanese 'rivals' – until the oil price skyrocketed. The rest is history.

This 'wait and see tactic' is frequently used by Chinese negotiators. Regular negotiators in China will be familiar with this scenario:

> Today the Chinese company wants to see a detailed plan for production. Tomorrow they ask for clarification and time to discuss the matter further. The following day, they make a request to revisit the production plant with a senior manager from their side. Meanwhile the potential foreign company is

eager to sign the deal. Head office is getting impatient. 'All we need is the Chinese signature,' say the Western negotiators. The Chinese want to discuss more details …

The Western company has put itself at a disadvantage by its haste. Maybe it has a notion of gaining a 'first mover advantage' – a most dubious benefit, especially when the Chinese, who have read their Sun Zi and their 36 Strategies, know that the company is desperate for it and can thus be manipulated via that desire. (Arguably 'first mover' is a weak strategy even if not played upon: Chinese companies are now advancing on early Western entrants in areas such as mobile phones and white goods.)

Deception in business can take many forms. Chinese may play at being innocent and ask for more and more information on your product. As a teacher, I've been asked for detailed outlines of my courses and even course materials, 'just so we can see what we are getting'. What they meant was 'so we can photocopy them and use them while telling you we're buying from someone else'. How do you get round that? You have to trust your intermediary. You must also establish in your own mind how much you are prepared to give. But remember too that you are at the start of a relationship, even though these guys are currently trying to pull wool over your eyes. Get to know them. If you can, offer them an invitation to the West. Court them.

Note that your competitors will probably be doing the same: in the end it will boil down to whether the company you are courting like you more than the others. Yes, this is a long process, but it is how business in China works.

Another ploy is secrecy, which can be used quite effectively by the Chinese in many negotiations. When you ask them for details, in search of specific buying signals – 'What is it that you are really looking for?' – you will get vague answers. This can be – no, it always is – infuriating. Don't fall into the trap of providing ever more detail about what you offer, to the point at which it can be stolen. Just take them out to another dinner.

Don't forget that from the Chinese perspective many Western businesses are unethical in their desire to make a fast buck without wishing to spend more time developing the business relationship or understanding the cultural mores.

As I have already highlighted, key, trust-based business relationships are the name of the game. Foreigners need to commit
themselves to a long-term approach of developing the necessary
contacts and persevering with them in the face of competition and
hurdles. If you are really earnest about the relationship and loyal
in sustaining it, you stand the best chance of being rewarded with
equal loyalty and trust. I know of one English business family who
have achieved this, and loyalty and trust has been passed on to the
next generations.

Luring the tiger from its lair

When I speak with Westerners about Chinese business strategies, they
can be dismissive and even rant on about how immoral some of the
Chinese approach to business discussions is. What they mean is that
the Chinese are not 'playing ball' by Western rules; the Chinese are
not easy to come to agreements with; the Chinese ask for too many
details about processes, procedures and products; they repeat requests
for certain items (and so on).

The upset Westerners are missing the point: these things are all part
of Chinese strategic thinking. The Chinese approach all negotiations
with a strategic mindset. Do not fool yourself that, because few of
them have been on MBA courses or speak managementese, they are
ill equipped: on the contrary, they will have been bought up on tales
of strategy. Having studied both Eastern and Western strategies, I find
the Eastern approaches much more subtle than Western ones. This
may be why they are perceived by Westerners as 'deceptive'.

Returning to the preconceptions noted at the start of this section, a
whole series of strategies has already been put into play by the Chinese
side. This is often done at an unconscious level: they are just seen as the
usual procedures in negotiation. Chinese companies competing with
one another adopt many of the classical Chinese military strategies
almost by instinct, each side being intuitively aware of the processes
involved.

Let us begin with the Chinese requirement for 'excessive' knowledge about the Western company. This is part of a strategy to size you
up and to estimate your ability to conduct a commercial battle. The
Chinese are following one of Sun Zi's strategic objectives, which is to
grasp the enemy's terrain. Master Sun sums this up when he says:

> Know your enemy, know yourself, and you can fight a
> hundred battles with no danger of defeat. When you are
> ignorant of the enemy but know yourself, your chances of
> winning and losing are equal. If you don't know either your
> enemy or yourself, you are bound to perish in all battles.

This passage shows a clear understanding of competitive intelligence. We know today that if a company can gain information about the strategic moves of its competitors, understand its customers and understand itself, it will gain the upper hand in the market. In a similar fashion, the Chinese are trying to gain the competitive advantage by understanding where the Western company is coming from. The purpose of obtaining as much information as possible about the 'enemy' is to win the commercial battle before it has begun. For Sun Zi, to win a battle by fighting is not the best strategy as it is costly in terms of human and material resources. For him the ideal scenario is summed up thus: 'to win a hundred victories in a hundred battles is not the culmination of skills. To subdue the enemy without fighting is the supreme excellence.'

The application of this principle of achieving victory without conflict in business means a company must win by *strategy*. If you start engaging in *tactical* warfare, such as cutting prices and giving discounts, then you have not won the war but are simply skirmishing. A true strategy would imply the use of an indirect approach to sustain your competitive advantage in the market without even confronting the competitor. For example, Microsoft has dominated the software market so utterly that there really are no competitors. Its strategy of out-competing its rivals has been amazingly successful. Of late, however, it has engaged in anti-competitive tactics which have resulted in lawsuits. Microsoft should stick to strategy: had it existed in Sun Zi's time, I am sure Bill Gates and his management team would have been admired by the master. In the Chinese context, another company that is winning the commercial battle without much conflict is the Starbucks franchise. Its strategic approach, focusing on just on a few major metropolitan centres in China with all the resources at its disposal, is paying dividends. Today, it is one of the most recognised brands in China, in spite of selling coffee for almost $2.50 per cup!

To illustrate another example of strategy at work, the Chinese will take advantage of the fact that China is now a 'hot' market for many global companies. They would make poor business strategists if they did not do this. Many other nations exploit such advantages (as with the strategic use of oil resources by some Middle Eastern countries). China is an almost irresistible lure, with its cheap labour force and vast potential internal market: the Chinese are bound to exploit this lure to the full. They would be crazy not to. As Sun Zi would say: 'Draw them in with the prospect of gain, take them by confusion.'

The way to 'take them by confusion' is to use deception strategies. These entail many tactics such as pretending not to know much about your company, appearing naïve and ignorant in the negotiation process, and using the standard approach of 'in China we do things like this'. In the process of appearing weak and lost, the Chinese are hoping to gain a psychological advantage over you. Sun Zi again sums it up: 'One with great skill appears inept.' This will make you overconfident and thus tempt you to expose your weaknesses, which will then be exploited to the full.

Please note that this is not done in a malicious tone or manner; it is part of the game to win tactical points and advantage. Indeed, most Chinese negotiators are very hospitable, polite and pleasant. You could be cynical and say this in itself is a strategic approach. You would probably be right – but remember that the Confucian rules of human interaction are at work here, too, and these are more important than any specific business transaction. Don't be too cynical – understand the rules!

Another strategic approach used by the Chinese in business negotiations is to invite you to a location of their choosing, whether this is their office premises or a resort outside Beijing or Shanghai. They will organise all the facilities and amenities to make your stay as comfortable and pleasant as possible. What is really happening is that you are being 'lured' to their terrain, which gives them the advantage. The approach comes straight from *The 36 Strategies*. Strategy 15, 'Luring the tiger out of the mountain' is designed to reduce the advantage of an adversary. In this case, the tiger is the adversary and the mountain represents its stronghold and home territory. The strategy must be to separate it from its lair.

The 36 Strategies gives a story based on the life of the Duke of Zheng, who lived at the end of the Zhou dynasty, about 2,800 years ago. The duke had a younger brother called Duan, who was keen to usurp his role, even though the duke was the rightful sovereign and had his father's blessing. The duke was aware of his brother's intentions, so created a strategy to lure him out of the capital city. He told Duan that he was going to visit the King of Zhou. When he left the city, his brother followed him with his army. Duan was falling into a trap. The duke did not go to see the King of Zhou, but simply wanted to be followed out of the capital. When Duan had reached a spot chosen by the duke as an ideal spot for an ambush, he found himself under attack. At the same time, any troops belonging to Duan who had been left in the city were also attacked. Duan was lured out of his stronghold and paid the consequences for his actions.

Applying this strategy to the business world, you may find yourself being lured away from Beijing or wherever you have your main office and support system, to visit a factory or to receive hospitality at a resort. This is strategy. You will be confined to a destination miles away from home and even from the capital cities in China. You may find yourself there for weeks with no decisions or results. You do not really speak the language; you are in an environment with a very different culture. The only entertainment will be DVDs, karaoke bars and more restaurants – enough to make you tear your hair out. At least you have not lost your head, like Duan.

The strategic reply is that the tiger must stay in its lair. Insist on having the meetings in major cities, on deciding all the schedules and on arranging all the amenities. It will cost you to do this, but the alternative is being outside your home ground, which could be far more expensive. Or why not play the Chinese game and invite the Chinese to visit you in your home base? You may need to pay fares and accommodation, but the advantages will be enormous. Now you are luring the Chinese tiger out of its lair.

Many foreign companies are already inviting Chinese delegations to visit their country. If you do this too, you will not only be securing a tactical advantage, but also building *guanxi* with the Chinese, hopefully showing them what excellent partners you will be (as well as simply providing them with something nice, for which they must be grateful). Given that few Chinese people have had much opportunity to travel overseas, this is an ideal opportunity for you to exploit your advantage.

Dishonest, or just strategic? I hope the above examples will help you to perceive things differently and therefore allow you to rethink the way you do business in China. The best strategy is to play the Chinese game by Chinese rules. Are you ready to invest the time and energy to understand these rules?

Corruption

As in any other emerging market, corruption is prevalent. In China's case, the situation has been exacerbated by the demise of the old socialist order laid down during Mao's reign. This left a huge cultural and moral vacuum, which has partially but not totally been filled by traditional Chinese culture. Added to this is the sudden new lure of great wealth.

The transition from a planned economy to a market economy offers particular opportunities for corrupt practices: this is not just a Chinese phenomenon. Many older Chinese feel overwhelmed by it, and look back longingly to the Mao era, when corruption was less of an issue. They conveniently forget there was no wealth to be corrupt about then.

The Chinese government is trying to tackle the problem. In the last five years 83,000 officials have been punished for corruption-related offences.

In some 'progressive' companies, people are being discouraged from using their *guanxi*, not always to the benefit of the business! A friend who works in the purchasing department of a Chinese enterprise recently installed new air conditioning units in the company. Instead of buying the cheaper Chinese models, which would have performed fine, he bought a much more expensive foreign brand. The reason was that he feared his peers would 'silently' accuse him of using his *guanxi* network if he had bought the Chinese ones. He did not want to be 'tainted with the corruption brush'.

For the Westerner seeking to do business in China, a key issue is related to paying for access to officials. Your intermediary will suddenly tell you that to see Secretary X or Mr Y, the key buyer in the local ministry, you need to pay him or her (the intermediary, not the ultimate contact) 10,000 renminbi. What do you do?

I am afraid I am a pragmatist here. I am Chinese. If you trust your intermediary – and if you do not trust your intermediary you are in deep, deep trouble – then that is the 'going rate'. The wheels of *guanxi* will be clanking round in ways you will probably never understand (this is not a straight bribe; people will have to be persuaded to open doors, which takes time and expenses such as dinners). Your job is to write out the cheque, then go and see the Secretary or Mr Y and ask for whatever it is you need. And to do so politely, in the spirit of a game.

Many Western commentators will throw up their hands in horror at my answer to this problem. I could reply with a comment about cultural imperialism, but I would rather avoid such arguments – they go nowhere – and get the job done.

It is illegal for nationals of some countries (such as America) to make payments *direct* to officials. You should know the law in your country. But the indirect route is different, and is taken time and time again by multinationals, by entrepreneurs, by individual consultants and others.

Suppose that you see the Secretary, that he is delightful and agrees to all your demands. Then a week later, your intermediary says there have been complications, and a further 5,000 renminbi is required.

Again, you just have to trust your intermediary. If the requests start becoming excessive, then the unwritten rules are probably being broken, and you will have to disengage. You have to make a judgement. Naturally, the longer you have been in China and the more people you know and trust, the easier it will be to make this judgement.

The legal system is also troubled with corruption. This is not a good thing, of course, but I cannot help feeling that avoidance of legal action should be a key business principle all round the world, so as a foreigner this is not your problem. In the West you may get a more objective judgment, but the legal fees will bankrupt you. In China, you at least have an alternative option: to use *guanxi* to negotiate your way round whatever problem threatens to end up in the courtroom.

The worst kind of corruption is the simple theft of money from Chinese institutions by their senior employees. The '59 phenomenon' has become common; officials have to retire at 60, and there have been many cases of people vanishing from their posts, and from China, with a large sum of money a year short of that age. This is probably the biggest corruption headache for the Chinese government, but affects SOEs much more than joint ventures. Luckily, you will not need to deal with it.

There is, of course, the issue of fraud and theft. This is not unknown in the West, and you should have procedures in place to prevent it. Had Barings Bank in Singapore been bought down by a conniving Oriental, no doubt reams of material about Chinese untrustworthiness would have been produced. Instead, the culprit came from Outer London.

China has a corruption problem, but the country is not, in my view, hopelessly corrupt, the way some nations are. It is not a 'kleptocracy'. You must be prepared to encounter corruption in China, but do not let its existence put you off doing business.

The Chinese are difficult to manage

MYTH

Chinese employees lack imagination, are inefficient, stupid (etc.). They have been featherbedded by years of Communism, which flattered their collective class vanity while at the same time smothering any capacity any particular individual might have had for initiative and responsibility.

REALITY

Chinese workers are diligent and smart.

They were, of course, poorly managed in the Communist era. During this period, Chinese managers in SOEs were driven by the need to meet quotas, the style of leadership was top down, and worker aspirations were not taken into account. In return, employees had the right to expect lifetime employment, health, education, pensions and accommodation: the 'iron rice bowl'. Rewards in the old system were based on seniority, age and (above all) on being a good political player. Managerial competence was not an issue.

Under the socialist government, Chinese workers were very demotivated and did not take the initiative in the workplace. People relied on 'someone else' to do the work, and often it never got done. This type of set-up is nicely illustrated in the saying: 'One monk has water to drink; two monks will probably have water to drink; three monks will have no water to drink'. The monk on his own will just go to the well and fetch the water for himself. If there are two monks, there is a temptation to expect the other guy to do it, but as he can directly blame you for being lazy, it is probably easiest to come to some kind of agreement such as splitting the task. With three monks, not only is it easy to assume 'someone else will do it', but there are enough individuals involved to make responsibility so diffuse that no one person will get blamed if nothing happens.

The attitude implicit in this story – that if you can get somebody else to do your work, you should – is still around in the Chinese workforce, especially in the SOE sector, though less so than in the apparently 'collective' Communist era. (I have noticed individuals with this philosophy in the West too.)

Given the long history of political dominance in all areas of Chinese life, it is not surprising that many employees, especially in SOEs, still think politically rather than economically. They would rather be 'politically correct' than organisationally efficient. The government does not help by sending mixed messages, pursuing a capitalist economic path but maintaining a Communist political ideology. What SOEs need now are clear, commercial value systems, with substantial and transparent rewards for meeting real business targets.

This is not just about the legacy of Communism, however. While much of the SOE management model was based on specifically Communist ideas, aspects of it stem naturally from older, more basic cultural assumptions, such as:

- The reverential tradition towards older people. This makes it difficult to suggest, let alone implement, new ways of doing things.

- Deference to authority. See the comment on power distance below.

- The tradition of paternalism. Do not forget that Confucian relationships had implications that fathers should protect and defend their families, as well as an expectation that they would be obeyed.

You will see more of these traits if you deal with SOEs, but they also manifest themselves in multinational joint venture companies, which supposedly have a more egalitarian culture.

Power distance in China

The term 'power distance' was coined by Mauk Mulder, an experimental psychologist, and popularised by Geert Hofstede in his classic work, *Cultures and Organizations*. In cultures with high power distance, subordinates expect to be led and do not question authority. In low power distance cultures, there is a culture of questioning authority. It will come as no surprise that China is a high power distance culture. (A veneer of egalitarianism, the relic of Communist rhetoric, exists – but it is wafer thin. Even Mao failed to narrow Chinese power distance: his 'Cultural Revolution' can be seen as a last, desperate attempt to achieve this impossible goal.)

Countries with low power distance include New Zealand, Scandinavia, Ireland and Austria. Oddly enough Taiwan is not as extreme as China in this respect, possibly due to the concentrated Western influence there, possibly because it is a smaller country, or because of its maritime traditions, or perhaps because of its long tradition of rebellion against mainland China (Formosan pirates were a notorious thorn in the side of mainland Chinese traders for many centuries; one of them, Koxinga, turned the island into an independent kingdom during the Qing dynasty).

Hofstede has a number of other metrics for cultures (his book is well worth reading, even though he does not seem to understand Confucianism very well, attributing to it an economic dynamism alien to the essentially aristocratic sage). One of these metrics is 'uncertainly avoidance'. The Daoist Chinese are happy with uncertainty. If you create a quadrant with power distance on one axis and uncertainly avoidance on the other, Chinese and other Asian cultures dominate the 'high power distance, low uncertainty avoidance' quadrant. Hofstede argues that each quadrant represents a style of structuring organisations. Anglo-Saxon organisations are responsive to markets; Germanic ones are like a 'well-oiled machine'; most countries go for large pyramidical structures. The Chinese are most like a family.

Confucius would be proud.

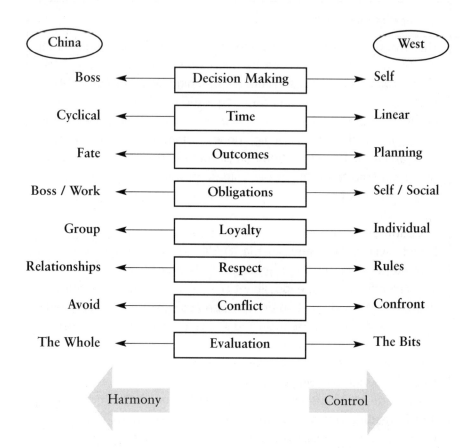

Figure 10.1 *Dilemmas of managing in China*

Figure 10.1 illustrates some of the dilemmas of managing in China, with the obvious differences in perceptions and assumptions about where each side is coming from. Managing a local workforce is one of the most challenging assignments in China, and it is in this area that I have heard many horror stories and disasters.

If you have read this far, you will know that there are plenty of ways things can go wrong. There are all the cultural and ethnic issues stemming from the fact that Chinese workers will be proud of their culture and identity, and probably defensive after hundreds of years of Opium Wars and other foreign incursions (and, for the older people, Communist anti-Western propaganda). Then there will be a lack of understanding of commercial issues (again, more of a problem with older workers). Finally there will be views of hierarchy – both in their duties and the company's responsibilities – that do not fit with what you learnt at business school or at work in the West. Add these all up and put under the pressure of a highly competitive market, and you can have a potentially explosive mixture!

In the rest of this chapter, we will consider some key issues.

Paternalism

The traditional Chinese management style is both sterner and more engaging than the Western one (of course, to Chinese, the Western style looks odd, with democratic rhetoric but no apparent care for the welfare of staff outside the workplace). Many Chinese worked in a *danwei* (work unit), which was the centre of their lives. It looked after their education and medical needs, organised cultural events, even arranged their funerals. (The nearest I can find to this in the Western tradition are paternalistic factories like Lever's Port Sunlight or Cadbury's Bournville. Even these fall short of the *danwei* model.)

Managing such an institution required not only strict discipline, but also 'winning the hearts of the staff'. To do so required a subtle balancing of how close one got to people. (Managers were helped by the Confucian tradition, whereby people expected this kind of leadership.) Many expatriates looking at Chinese managers see the 'hard' or ruthless side of the Chinese leader only, and miss the 'soft' or caring side, which is often expressed after work hours. A Chinese manager will talk about a worker's personal issues and his family affairs, and, most importantly in China, invite them to a restaurant for a meal.

Western managers face dilemmas that are not faced by their Chinese counterparts. Local staff may well not tolerate a dictatorial approach from a Westerner, although they have accepted one from a Chinese manager. This is partly due to historical and ethnic factors, but the same can also apply for overseas Chinese managers: recently I heard of a Chinese employee who was so disgusted by her treatment at the hands of a Hong Kong manager that she destroyed data on computer files.

Underneath this thinking is the Confucian notion of family. The *danwei* was effectively a large Chinese family, with all its reciprocal duties and obligations. Over and above that, China is one big family. Coming in from outside requires a huge mental shift.

Politeness

Chinese staff tend to tell you what you want to hear. I have already discussed the unreliability of national and provincial statistics, but the same is true of management information generally. This is partially about self-protection, but also stems from the cultural imperative of preserving harmony.

This is a difficult issue: the Chinese have problems with it themselves. One obvious way round it is wherever possible to get more than one source of information. Check behind the scenes. If faced by perfect sales figures, how much stock is left?

In the long run, the solution has to be to instil a culture of openness and truth telling. This can be done in various ways. I know of one company that simply used a big stick: submit incorrect figures and you are fired. A more subtle approach involves winning people round. Part of the motive for this kind of deception is fear, so make it clearer that telling the truth will be rewarded not punished. Make role models of people who practice openness.

Of course this is a long-term process, but an effective one, as research has shown. At the heart of good management in China is to be a good teacher, an educator – something that is highly valued by Chinese in all areas of life including the workplace.

Fitting in

Many Western managers are unlikely to have a command of the Chinese language. This can be a major barrier to management effectiveness. Although all staff in joint venture companies need English as an entry requirement, the level of fluency varies enormously.

It is still possible to communicate effectively by other methods. For example, here is the story of an American friend of mine called Tony, who worked in China for many years. Tony was an unassuming person of about 40 years old who was the IT manager of a section of his company. He did not speak Mandarin, but made efforts by attending some evening classes; he found it tough, on top of all his other work, but at least he was seen to try. He showed a lot of respect and affection for his Chinese staff, and this was reciprocated. Although he lived in expatriate housing, he tended not to mix much with the expatriate community, who he felt were always complaining about China and not really giving their best shot at really understanding the country's culture and idiosyncrasies. During his daily routines at work he used every opportunity to engage with his staff and try to understand what made the Chinese 'tick'. Tony took meticulous care and adjusted his communication style according to each individual's interest, needs, personality and position in the company. When the opportunity arose, he would invite his 15 staff to dinner at his place, although I am sure the Chinese would expect less tasty food there! Such gestures were greatly appreciated by his staff and endeared him to them – remember food is a symbol of friendship and a powerful channel to improve relationships. He also attended the wedding of one of his staff and regularly had beers with his team. Despite his lack of Mandarin, he created great loyalty among his subordinates, and they responded by putting in extra effort at critical times.

Managing in China is a challenge even to the most experienced global manager, but persistence, efforts to understand a totally different culture, sharing in activities and patience will yield success. Here is what a senior manager of a European global company, who has been in China for nine years, has to say. He leads by example and mentors his managers, and I believe this is the future direction for managing Chinese staff.

My assistant, Mary, had worked for six years in the company before I became her boss. Generally, she did what she was asked to do and little more. When I became her boss, I made it very clear to her that I expected her to use her initiative and to make her own decisions, at first, of course, with my help and guidance. Later, she came to fully understand my methods, motives and sense of humour. Now, she is probably the best assistant manager in the company. She is fully motivated and loves her job. We manage my China team together. There are times when I concede to her understanding and ways of dealing with issues, and other times when we discuss together which will be the best way to deal with an issue: Chinese way, Western way or a mixture of both. This way, we share our experiences and knowledge: she learns about us and I learn about the Chinese. Together we decide who will handle which issue/person and we decide together: there is no autocracy. For example, recently, she had to fire one of my staff who was under her. He was 49 years old and a foreigner. We discussed it beforehand and both agreed that I would do the firing but with her present and contributing to the meeting. It worked perfectly: the job got done, but face was preserved. Mary says that she is receiving an excellent education in management. I have a fantastic assistant.

Cultural bias in Western management methods

The nature of Western management concepts/techniques has made it difficult for Western managers to manage in China. Not all Western management technology is neutral; it has a cultural bias that can hinder adoption, especially in 'soft' skills such as such as human resource management and marketing. (Western models of 'hard' skills are perceived as being less of a cultural threat.)

Many Western management concepts – hard and soft – are based on values and assumptions from a post-industrial society. For example, notions such as assertiveness and 'empowerment' are not compatible with the current behavioural patterns and incentives prevalent in Chinese society.

The aim for good managers in China should be to adapt Western methods to local conditions, rather than to impose them and risk rejection and alienation among staff.

Team-working

This notion is perceived very differently by the Chinese. There the attitude is that senior managers should know their roles and responsibilities and should have the 'answers' to problems, otherwise they should not be managers in the first place.

At the same time, an employee who makes an innovative suggestion will probably be perceived by Chinese line managers as someone who is very ambitious and wants to usurp their position as well as to make them lose face. Thus the notion of sharing problems and finding solutions together with senior management is contrary to current cultural values. Instead, there will be a reluctance to make even a constructive criticism of someone in authority.

Much of this attitude stems from the educational system in China, where criticising the teacher is frowned on. The educational system still imbues the principle of 'one right way': one, and only one, correct solution to a problem. This is in contrast to Western management whereby there are general principles and tools/techniques to apply in any context.

The best way round this problem is to give everyone clear roles within the team, and then gradually move towards a Western, debate-driven model. Too much debate too early will achieve nothing.

Initiative

'Chinese managers lack initiative' is an old saw. It is probably still true in many cases – though I have noticed a number of Western managers not exactly overflowing in this department! The question is, of course, how to get round this problem. I suggest several approaches:

- Tell everybody what they are supposed to be achieving and why. Much initiative is destroyed by people not having a clear vision of what they are supposed to be doing: they stick to the 'rule book' in absence of any larger principles.

- Send out clear signals. Praise and reward initiative. Chinese are used to having role models held up to them: the Communists did so, ad nauseam, with characters like the Good Soldier Lei Feng. Praise people in the business who have taken initiatives and succeeded, cite successful Chinese entrepreneurs from outside the company, such as the CEO of Haier.

- Do not shame people if initiative fails. This is the best way to demotivate imaginative individuals.

Feedback

The whole notion of face militates against having a good feedback system. People will say what they expect you want to hear, or what you should hear to keep that Confucian harmonious whole. Suggestions that may help to mitigate this problem are:

- One-to-one sessions are much more likely to generate sincerity than group ones.

- Keep an ear open for gossip. Formal communication is dominated by considerations of 'face', but informal communication can be a lot freer. The problem, of course, is that it is unreliable, and so can only be used as part of a process.

- Begin the session with technical questions, and work towards more personal topics.

Attitudes of Western managers
It is also important that Western managers look at themselves and their assumptions. They can present an idealised version of Western organisations. Perhaps a degree of *unlearning* is required. Expatriate managers could share some critical analysis of the companies in the West such as Enron and WorldCom. The experience of these companies in dealing with corporate corruption has interesting parallels with companies in China.

Expatriate managers also need to be clear what their mission is in China. Quite a few of the ones I have met have been naive about this. From the Chinese perspective, they are there to transfer knowledge. A good expatriate should accept this, and train Chinese subordinates to take over the top positions, providing coaching and sending them regularly back to headquarters for further training or experience. For bright Chinese, training is critical to their choice of which jobs to take. Many Chinese managers I know would be willing to sacrifice higher pay and status to get the training that would improve future prospects. For example, I know a very smart and savvy Chinese manager who took a position with a company because they were prepared to sponsor her MBA training; she took a pay cut and loss of status in process, but was happy to do so.

Cross-cultural training
There is an assumption by quite a few expatriate managers in China that the keys to success are twofold and simple: specialist functional knowledge and international experience. But there is a third, essential aspect: cultural understanding. On many occasions I have come across expatriate managers who have not had any form of cultural training, or at best

merely half a day. Their knowledge of Chinese culture and history was either non-existent or so abysmally low as to be of no use to them.

In my view it is absolutely crazy to spend millions of dollars investing in China without giving managers time to invest in cultural training. Local Chinese do not expect encyclopedic knowledge of Chinese culture and mores, simply sufficient knowledge and understanding. An expatriate friend who has spent five years in China made the following comment:

> One's first year in China is spent in wide-eyed wonderment; the second year is spent trying to get a fix on it all. By the end of the second year, we think we have the place understood. By the end of the third year, we realise that we know nothing and it is only then, after three years and once we accept how little we really know, that we truly start to learn about and understand China.

Many companies send expatriates to China on a three-year 'mission': just when these people are at the point when they can start to be really valuable, they are sent somewhere else.

Sourcing managers

Many foreign companies employ overseas Chinese managers from Taiwan, Singapore, Hong Kong or the United States. This does at least avoid problems caused by ignorance of language and cultural heritage. But I have already discussed difficulties with this approach. The local workforce do not always experience the fellow-feeling they are supposed to, especially if the overseas Chinese managers are actually not very good but have been given the job because of their ethnicity. In my experience, Chinese would prefer good Caucasian managers to such people.

A better solution has been to employ 'returnee' managers: Chinese who have been educated in the West and perhaps had some experience of working in developed economies. These people have a relatively good understanding of how Western organisations work, and of the Western business culture and mindset. They are also more openly ambitious and 'business savvy' than people educated in China. At the same time they have a thorough, natural grasp of Chinese culture and language, and the ability to utilise the *guanxi* network.

Such talent does not come cheap. I know a returnee who has

accepted a position with a huge mining multinational at a salary that is very high even by British or European standards, given his age and business experience. Although only 36 years old, he was really recruited for his *guanxi* connections and to negotiate his way through the Chinese bureaucracy, as the mining sector is a pillar industry in China and has a lot of bureaucratic involvement. My guess is this will prove an excellent investment.

Such appointments can create friction with the local workforce: locally educated Chinese may be envious that a returnee has relatively higher status and is being paid so much more for what they consider they could do equally well. The returnee has to prove him or herself.

Retaining key local staff

There is a chronic shortage of qualified and experienced managers in China across all sectors. This means that good managers are beginning to increase their demands, and that big companies – both foreign and Chinese – are going along with this. Mobility is increasing. It has been estimated that companies in China have annual turnover rates of about 11.5 per cent, which is about three times the global average (according to Hewitt Associates (2003)). How can a company keep its best people?

In addition, many Chinese would rather run their own business than be part of someone else's. As an old Chinese saying goes, 'I'd rather be the head of a chicken than the tail of an ox'.

Foreign companies can have an advantage here: many Chinese still prefer to work for foreign companies, even if wages are a little less than in Chinese ones, because they like the working ambience, attitudes to staff and the opportunities for further advancement (not necessarily just in China). Foreign companies can build on this advantage by:

- Developing and institutionalising a deep understanding of Chinese society and values.

- Offering an 'all-round' benefits package. China's social security system is woefully inadequate: health care may be cheap but its quality leaves much to be desired. Offer your skilled staff health insurance and other welfare benefits. In effect you are reinventing Chairman Mao's iron rice bowl, though now for senior managers – a platinum rice bowl, perhaps?

- Leveraging the 'family' concept by employing your staff's relatives or partners. Such practices may be frowned upon in the West as smacking of 'nepotism': in China it simply enhances the all-important connections between your people and company.

CONCLUSION

Having said all this, many Chinese managers and workers are very keen to learn, change and improve for the future. The Chinese see this as a powerful way of increasing China's competitiveness in the world market, and they are very fast learners.

Given that many Western management techniques are new to Chinese employees, it is essential that the staff absorb, digest and engage with the ideas in debate before they begin to adapt and apply them. This is unlikely to happen in a workplace where modern Western management thinking is seen as aggressively attacking the dominant traditional Chinese cultural values. The more you can dovetail the two, the easier it will be to create 'management with Chinese characteristics' which will be happily taken up and used by Chinese workers and managers.

If you want the respect of Chinese subordinates, be polite and understand Chinese culture and ways as much as you can. Have humility about the fact that you are an outsider and have a lot to learn about the culture.

It also helps to be clever! Not necessarily academic, though academic achievement is highly admired, but smart. If you can set a good example of getting things done effectively and imaginatively, you will be admired.

Good managers in China are flexible. This is not a new notion; in good Chinese style, I shall 'prove' the point by quoting an age-old authority. Sun Zi advised commanders, 'do not repeat the tactics that won you a victory, but vary them according to circumstances'.

In the end, what Chinese workers want is good management: people who are expert, respected within the company and educated about China and its ways.

Afterword

Writing this book has been demanding emotionally. I have had to face up to a number of unattractive aspects of my own culture, including xenophobia and corruption. Business in China is hard.

I would not like to leave readers with a picture of an unremitting grind, however. China's is one of the great cultures of the world, offering the West a whole range of fresh philosophical and spiritual perspectives and artistic experiences. Doing business in China and coming to know its culture better must go hand in hand, and should be rewarding and exciting – just as I have enjoyed learning throughout my life about the West and its ways. If you cultivate a fascination for and a delight in China, its history and culture, you will find doing business here easier. You will also find, when the going gets tough, that there is much to be enjoyed along the way.

Appendix A
A summary of key success factors for dealing with the Chinese

- Learn the rules to play the game in the China market – understand the business culture.

- You need 'insider status'. Develop *guanxi*. You need to be plugged into the government and the business network – to be informed, to anticipate changes in the regulatory landscape, to spot opportunities and to get things done.

- Spend time finding the appropriate Chinese partner. Conduct a thorough due diligence on the partner company, as well as making sure it shares the same agenda. Otherwise, you may face the situation aptly put in a Chinese saying of 'sharing the same bed but having different dreams'.

- Build up a critical mass of market knowledge. China is highly fragmented, and the more knowledge you have about the different sectors and players, the greater the chances of success.

- Do not become over fixated on China's challenges to the point of devising only strategies to counter threats and ignoring the potential opportunities.

- Have a compelling business value proposition and a simple business model. Research indicates that those companies with a manageable business model – such as focusing only on core business activities that build competitive advantage – are likely to succeed. The philosophy is to '*start small with overwhelming force before expanding*'.

- Have a long-term perspective: China is not one of those 'get rich quick' markets ...

- ... but if you can have a short-term success too, that is good. Chinese partners like to be associated with 'winners' who will enhance their status.

- Set clear goals. Companies must know just *what* and *how much* they expect to achieve in China and over *what time period*.

- Be flexible in responding to changes in markets, regulations, etc. The Chinese are very practical people and will adapt with you.

Appendix B
Some key differences between China and the West

China	The West
Historical and political context	
Very populous country.	Low/middle population density.
Frontiers open but dangerous (northern barbarians) or closed (seas, mountains).	Frontier open and ready for exploration/conquest.
Need to protect existing land from invasion or natural disaster.	Need to create or improve land.
Need for vast armies or project teams.	Rush for land, or prosperity created by initiative of innovative individuals.
Need for hierarchy: armies or project teams must be controlled centrally.	Hierarchies get in the way.
Small controlling elite, plus large, undifferentiated peasant/soldier (later, worker) masses – *lao bai xing*.	Market society develops: class structure more subtle, with all sorts of people at different levels.

Simple class-based analysis (Mao) resonated.	Simple class-based analysis ridiculous.
Strong ideology of social harmony.	Strong ideology of perpetual progress.
Change seen as cyclical: Yin becomes Yang, reverts to Yin again (and so on).	Change has a direction.

Authority

Respect for authority per se.	Authority must earn respect, or it is invalid.
Respect for age and experience.	Cult of youth.
Teachers venerable.	Teachers 'ladders to be discarded'.

Individuality

Individual meaningless on own. (Daoist escape route for loners).	Individuality essential, the point of it all. Alternatives inauthentic, 'flight from freedom'.
But people still need to define and protect themselves! So ...	You make your own definition and find your own protection (law a source of protection).

Family

... Family – *jiaren* – at the heart of who you are.	Family of origin can be a burden that needs to be escaped.
Includes extended family.	Extended family broken up.

Family held together by duty (see below).	Nuclear family united by love (until divorce...).

Friendship

Friendship – *zijiren, shuren* – second line of defence. Close, long-term, trust-based.	Friendship important, but not as important as in China. No clear definition of what 'friendship' is.
Rules of friendship clear.	Rules of friendship undefined.
Lifelong exchange of favours (including borrowing or lending money).	Exchange of favours unimportant (and slightly frowned on, e.g. borrowing money off a friend).
Friendship based on time and 'good maintenance'.	Friendship based on affection.
Webs of interconnected people are delicate and must not be disturbed.	Rolodexes change frequently. Americans particularly mobile.

Conflict

Distaste for personal conflict.	Conflict lets off steam.
Where there is conflict, it is massive.	

Character

Displays of emotion discouraged, denote indiscipline.	Emotional repression regarded as inauthentic, denotes shiftiness.
Expectation that people will read subtle signals.	Value of honesty and openness.

Your fault if you do not interpret properly.	Your fault if you do not communicate properly.
'Hidden depth'.	WYSIWYG.
Lin Daiyu.	Madonna.

Business practice

Trust-based.	Contract-based, deal-based.
Relationship develops over time.	One-off deals fine.
Negotiations slow…	Get to agreement as soon as you reasonably can.
…and formal. Informality seen as threatening.	Informality a sign of progress.
Deception an acceptable part of strategic armoury.	Deception unacceptable, a sign that someone is fundamentally untrustworthy.
Contracts 'gestures of trust' which remain negotiable.	Contract a fixed point of certainty.

Time

Slow – 'What's a year in a man's life?'	Fast – 'Time is money'.
Cyclical – rise and fall of dynasties.	Progressive – 'continuous improvement', 'Whig' model of history.
Lumpy – Zen/Daoist cultivation of special enlightened moments.	Atomic – clock time, to be parcelled out as efficiently as possible.

Duty

Duty to other people, to specific individuals (or at least to individuals with specific social roles).	Duty to abstract principles.

Governing principles

Rule of man.	Rule of law.
Hierarchy the governing social principle.	Law the governing social principle.
Reductio ad absurdam: Maoist Mass Line. 'Obey actions in all your actions.'	*Reductio ad absurdam*: alienation from society and even self. David Hume: 'I am nothing but a bundle of sensations.'

Appendix C
Making sense of Pinyin

Pinyin is the system by which Chinese characters are translated into the Western alphabet – or more precisely, how the sounds of the characters are so translated. It is not the only such system, which is why people used to talk about Pekin, Peking, Peiping and now Beijing.

Some simple rules will help you start to pronounce Chinese names correctly. Most pinyin follows sensible rules: Shanghai is pronounced 'Shang-hai', simple as that! It becomes more complicated with certain consonants:

Q is pronounced Ch (so the Qing dynasty is pronounced 'ching').
X is pronounced Sh (so the city of Xian is pronounced 'Shee-an').
Zh is pronounced J (so Sun Zhongshan is pronounced 'Jong-shan').
C on its own is pronounced Ts (so the word for food, *cai*, is pronounced 'tsai').

Vowels and diphthongs to note include:

-ian is pronounced 'yen'.
-eng is pronounced '-ung'.
-ong is pronounced '-ung', with a short, Yorkshire u.
-ou is pronounced '-oe' so Zhou Enlai was 'Joe'.
-ui is pronounced 'way', so Guilin, famous for its river scenery, is 'Gway-lin'.
-i (on its own) is a trap, being pronounced -ee is some cases and as a kind of -rr sound in others. The 'ee' is more common, but the syllable *shi* has hundreds of meanings, including 'to be' and is pronounced 'shrr'.

Beyond all this, of course, lie the intricacies of tone. The same sylla-ble can have totally different meanings, depending on the tone. *Ai* for example, can mean 'Oh dear', dust, the angstrom unit, cancer, white, to suffer, haze, short, narrow, to obstruct, love ... This is beyond the scope of this book, however.

Appendix D
Recommended reading

Over the years I have read many books on the subject of the West and China. A longer list follows, but I would like to suggest a short reading list for busy but curious executives.

Inside Chinese Business by Ming-Jer Chen provides an excellent overview of broad cultural issues and of the minutiae of etiquette.

Please read either Sun Zi's *Art of War* or *The 36 Strategies* – or both if you have time. *The Romance of the Three Kingdoms* is a classic historical novel that is full of stories of Chinese strategy and counter-strategy.

Michael Bond's *Beyond the Chinese Face* is a little academic, but has interesting material, especially about socialisation.

There are many books on Chinese history; *The Search for Modern China* by Jonathan D. Spence is recommended.

The *Lonely Planet* and *Rough Guides* to China have excellent introductions, as well as the usual useful travellers' info.

For a quick read, J. C. Yang's *Xenophobe's Guide to the Chinese* made me laugh and had a few truths to hit home. What I would really like to see is a companion guide, to Westerners.

Literary-minded readers should read *Hong Lou Meng* (*The Dream of Red Mansions*, sometimes known as *The Story of the Stone*). This classic Qing dynasty novel will tell you all you need to know about the Chinese notion of family and its importance, and also show the exquisite and fragile sensibilities behind often cold, public faces. The work is long – people had more time to sit and read in the Qing dynasty – and slow. Too slow for many modern readers. My advice is not to expect to finish it, but if you read just one of the five volumes, or even a hundred pages or so of it, you will gain immense insight.

And if you fall in love with it, as some readers do, you will carry on and read to the end, all 1,000 or more pages!

Western novelists often make a good fist of understanding China (and have the advantage of writing in a style that is aimed at Western readers). Crime fans should, of course, read Chris West's *China Quartet*, about a Beijing-based police inspector. Start with *Death of a Blue Lantern*. For adventure readers, James Clavell's China novels capture East–West misunderstanding excellently. Literary readers should try the Nobel Prize-winning *The Good Earth* by Pearl S. Buck – it is a bit out of fashion now, but she knew the old China well.

Bibliography

Ambler, T. and Witzel, M. (2004) *Doing Business in China*. London, Routledge.

Blackman, C. (2000) *'China Business' The rules of the game*. Sydney, Allen & Unwin.

Bond, M. H. (1991) *Beyond the Chinese Face: Insights from Psychology*. Hong Kong, Oxford University Press.

Brahm, L. J (2003) *When YES means NO!* Boston, Tuttle.

Bucknall, K. (1994) *Cultural Guide to Doing Business in China*. Oxford, Butterworth-Heinemann.

Chang, G. (2002) *The Coming Collapse of China*. London, Century Publications.

Chen, Ming-Jer (2001) *Inside Chinese Business*. Boston, Harvard Business School Press.

Chu, Chin-Ning (1991) *The Asian Mind Game*. New York, Rawson.

Cleary, T. (1988) *Sun Tsu's Art of War*. Boston, Shambhala.

Cleary, T. (1999) *Ways of the Warriors, Codes of Kings: Lessons in leadership from the Chinese Classics*. Boston, Shambhala.

Crow, C. (1937) *400 Million Customers*. New York, Halcyon.

Economy, E. C. (2004) *The River Runs Black: The Environmental Challenge to China's Future*. Ithaca, Cornell University Press.

Fang, T. (1999) *Chinese Business Negotiating Style*. Thousand Oaks CA, Sage.

Goodfellow R., Wang, K. and Sheng, Z. X. (1998) *Chinese Business Culture*. Oxford, Butterworth-Heinemann.

Griffith, S. B. (1963) *Sun Tzu: The Art of War*. New York, Oxford University Press.

Hall E. T. and Hall M. R. (1990) *Understanding Cultural Differences.* Yarmouth ME, Intercultural Press.

Hofstede, G. (1994) *Cultures and Organizations.* London, HarperCollins Business.

Hewitt Associates (2003) *Workforce Management*, pp. 28–33.

Hou, W. C. and Luh, L. L. (1998) *The 36 Strategies of the Chinese.* Singapore, Addison Wesley Longman.

Kenna, P. and Lacy, S. (1994) *Business China: A Practical Guide to Understanding Chinese Business Culture.* New York, Contemporary Publishing House.

Kirkbride, P. S., Tang, S. F. and Westwood, R. I. (1991) Chinese Conflict Preferences and Negotiating Behaviour: Cultural and Psychological Influences. *Organisation Studies,* **12**(3): 365–86

KPMG (2003) *Business Week*, 3rd November.

Li, C. (1998) *China: The Consumer Revolution.* Singapore, Wiley.

Redding, S. G. (1993) *The Spirit of Chinese Capitalism.* Berlin, de Gruyter.

Seligman, S. (2000) *Dealing with the Chinese.* London, Management Books.

Sia, A. (1997) *The Chinese Art of Leadership.* Singapore, Asiapac.

West, C. (1999) *Journey to the Middle Kingdom.* London, Allison and Busby.

West, C. (2002) *The Beermat Entrepreneur.* London, Prentice Hall.

West, C. (2005) *The Boardroom Entrepreneur.* London, Random House.

Index

36 Strategies, 94, 96, 97, 112–13,
116–17
  categories, 96
  Strategy 4, 112
  Strategy 12, 96
  Strategy 15, 116
  Strategy 27, 96
  see also strategies
400 Million customers, 49

A

Academy of Social Sciences, 59
Accenture, 41
advertising, 8, 12, 32
Africans, prejudice against, 75
Agricultural Bank of China, 23
agriculture and farming, 14, 16–17,
  19
AIG, 63
Alcatel, 32, 111
Americans, prejudice by, 75
Amway, 37
animal rights, 111
Art of War (Bing Fa), 78, 94–6,
  97
authority, 34, 45, 46, 52, 99, 107,
  122, 123, 129, 133,
  key differences between China
    and the West, 140

automotive industry, 12, 16, 17–18,
  63, 112
  see also individual car
    manufacturers
Avic, 69
Avon, 37

B

Bank of China, 23
banking, 14, 15, 16, 18, 22–7
  guanxi as, 70
  system characteristics, 23–5
  theft from banks, 24, 120
bankruptcy, 18, 20, 36
Bao Shu Ya, 84–5
bargaining, 37, 48, 93, 102, 112
  see also negotiation; restaurants
Barings Bank, 120
Beijing, 4, 7, 8, 16, 22, 23, 24, 29,
  35, 37, 43, 59, 60, 69, 72, 73,
  76, 80, 89, 116
Beijing National Economic
  Research Institute, 16
biotechnology, 111
Book of Changes (Yi-jing, known as
  I Ching in the West), 54, 55
Book of Odes (Shi-jing), 54
border disputes, 72
Buddhism, 78

bureaucracy, 2, 4, 8, 21, 32–7, 41,
   62, 94, 100, 132
   characteristics, 35–6
   see also state-owned enterprises
business cards, 52–3, 94
business consultants, 41, 42
   see also guanxi
Business Link, UK, 42
business markets, 30, 137
   electronic goods, 30, 31
   see also mobile phone sector
business practice, 105–20
   key differences between China
      and the West, 142

C
Cadbury, 125
Cadence Design Systems, 109
Cao Cao, 81–2
capital, Chinese use of, 13, 18, 33,
   37–8
   management, 37–8
Captaino, 68–9
Carrefour, 38
CBBC (China–Britain Business
   Council), 41
CBRC (China Banking Regulatory
   Commission), 23
CCTV (China Central Television),
   65
Chang, Gordon, 24
change in China, 57–8
Changhong televisions, 32
Chen Kaige, 47
children, 46–7, 56, 57–8, 59–60,
   73, 83, 90
   see also one-child policy
children born outside marriage
   (sishengzi), 59
China Banking Regulatory
   Commission (CBRC), 23

'China bashing', 57, 73, 75–6
   see also prejudice
China–Britain Business Council
   (CBBC), 41
China Central Television (CCTV), 65
China Construction Bank, 23
China Daily, 41
'China Fever', 5, 39
China Telecom, 12
Chinese Academy for Social
   Sciences, 6
Chinese New Year, 51
Citroen, 18
Ci Xi, Dowager Empress, 79
Clark, Donald (Washington
   University), 37
Coming Collapse of China, 24
communication, 4, 74, 82, 84–5,
   85–91, 126, 130
   in high-context cultures, 86–9
   in low-context cultures, 86–9
   in the work environment, 37,
      83, 89–91, 126–7, 129
   see also emotions; languages
Communism, 3, 49, 72, 121, 122
Communist Party, 48, 79
compromise, 100, 102, 103
concubines, 59
   see also women
conflict, 55, 83–4, 97, 101, 115,
   124
   key differences between China
      and the West, 141
Confucianism, 3, 44, 45–58, 94,
   106, 107, 116, 123, 125, 129
   face (mianzi), 48–53
   key differences between China
      and the West, 141–2
   losing, 50–2, 53
   preserving, 51, 52–3, 62, 67,
      90, 94, 128

family, 125
harmony (*hexie/hemu*), 45, 50,
    53–6, 62, 83–4, 94, 102, 103,
    124, 126
person of quality (*junzi*), 45, 56–7
relationships/responsibility, 45–7
    elder–younger, 46
    father–son (parent–child), 45,
        46–7
    friend–friend, 46
    husband–wife, 46, 47
    ruler–subject, 45
values, 3, 45, 62, 107
Confucius (Kong Fuzi), 1, 44, 45,
    56, 78, 94, 110, 123
see also Confucianism
consumer product sectors, 8
continuing boom scenario, 14
contracts, 86, 93, 98, 103, 104,
    111, 142
corruption, 18, 20, 24, 25, 27, 35,
    39, 62, 75, 79, 105, 106, 108,
    118–20, 130
'59 phenomenon', 119–20
counterfeiting, 35–6, 72, 106, 107,
    110
see also intellectual property
    rights
credit, 37
control systems in banks, 23
criticism, of an individual, 90
Crocodile, 68–9
Crow, Carl, 49
cuisine, *see* culinary areas
culinary areas, 7–8
cultural assumptions/issues, 2, 43,
    44, 50, 58, 84, 93, 94, 100,
    101, 106, 107, 109, 110, 118,
    122, 123, 125, 126, 127, 128,
    130, 131, 132, 133
see also cultures

cultural history, 2, 3, 32, 33, 44,
    45, 58, 71, 77–80, 89, 94, 118,
    131
see also Confucianism; prejudice
Cultural Revolution, 44, 50, 78,
    107, 123
cultural training, 130–1
cultural understanding, 62, 67, 74,
    75, 89–90, 94, 106, 109, 130–1
Cultures and Organizations, 123
cultures
differences, 4, 29–42, 100, 107,
    117
    Northerners and Southerners, 4
    coastal versus inland, 5
    rural versus urban, 5
    high/low context, 86–8
    high/low power distance, 123

D

danwei (work unit), 125–6
Dao de Jing, 82
Daoism, 53, 82, 94, 97, 102, 123,
    140, 142
Da Shan (CCTV), 65
decentralisation of power, 35
see also state-owned enterprises
deception in business, 19, 95, 96,
    106, 113, 114, 116, 126, 142
Dell Computers, 31
Deng Xiaoping, 4, 58, 80
Department of Trade and Industry
    (DTI), UK, 41
UK Trade and Industry, 42
Development Research Council,
    106
dialects, 3, 4
diplomacy in business, 52, 56
distribution systems, 38
divorce, 60
domestic market, 40

Dream of Red Mansions, 64, 85
DTI *see* Department of Trade and
    Industry
duty, key differences between China
    and the West, 143
dynasties, 45, 78, 89, 142
  Han, 44, 78, 81
  Ming, 77, 78, 79
  Qing, 60, 79, 123, 145, 147
  Shang, 77, 78, 79
  Song, 33, 78
  Sui, 78
  Tang, 47, 78
  Xia, 77
  Yuan, 78
  Zhou, 78, 116

E
East India Company, 71
economy, Chinese, 1, 2, 4, 12, 16,
    17, 18, 21, 22, 27, 35, 38, 73,
    122, 123, 131
  development, 2, 5, 9, 11–12, 13,
      16, 17, 20, 25, 27, 32, 39, 44,
      62, 80, 95, 118
  growth, 11, 12, 13, 14, 17, 19,
      21, 26, 27, 31
  scenarios, 14, 26–7
    continuing boom, 14
    meltdown, 14–15
    slowdown, 14
  see also growth
Economy, Elizabeth, 16
education, 17, 20, 47–8, 56, 57, 64,
    83, 106, 125, 129
embarrassment, 51, 56, 90–1
emotions, 48, 56, 82, 90–1, 102,
    141
  see also inscrutability
energy consumption, 17, 19
Enron, 130

environmental problems, 15, 16,
    17, 44
etiquette, social, 48, 51, 52, 56, 57,
    94, 100
  see also cultural assumptions/
      issues; cultural understanding
examinations, 83, 94, 106, 110–11
expatriates, 22, 39, 52, 66, 72, 73,
    75, 76, 125, 127, 130, 131
  see also foreigners; Westerners
eye contact, 91

F
F1 *see* Formula One
Fabius (Roman general), 112
face (*mianzi*) *see* Confucianism, face
family (*jiaren*), 14, 44–5, 57–8,
    59–60, 65, 74, 123, 125–6, 133
  key differences between China
      and the West, 140–1
  see also guanxi
Fan Juanfen, 68–9
fathers, 46–7, 54, 60, 122
  see also husbands; paternalism
FDI *see* foreign direct investment
feedback in business, 88, 129–30
Fisher, George (CEO, Kodak), 34
flooding, 15
food, 99, 119, 127
  arrival times for meals, 89
  see also culinary areas; friendship;
      restaurants
Forbidden City, 72
Ford, 18, 40, 63, 112
foreign direct investment (FDI), 11
foreigners, 66, 71, 72, 76, 77, 88,
    102, 114
  categories of, 66
  see also expatriates; Westerners
Foreign Office, UK, 41
foreign reserves, 12

formality, 90–1, 100, 130, 142
Formosan pirates, 123
Formula One (F1), 29
Fortune 500, 110
friendship (*zijiren*, *shuren*), 45, 46,
    48–56, 61, 65–6, 68, 84–5,
    90–1, 99, 127
  breakdown of, 53, 84
  key differences between China
    and the West, 141
  power of, 84–5
  see also guanxi
Fu Manchu, 81–91
Fuji, 31

G
Galanz, 30, 31
Gates, Bill, 115
Gatorade, 8
GBCC (Great Britain–China
    Centre), 41
General Electric, 40
General Motors (GM), 12, 18, 40,
    63, 112
Giordano, 38
GM *see* General Motors
governing principles, key differences
    between China and the West,
    143
government, 9, 11, 25, 34, 35, 43,
    69, 89, 93, 118, 119, 121, 122
  decentralisation, 35
Great Britain–China Centre
    (GBCC), 41
'Great Leap Forward' campaign, 19
Greenberg, Hank (CEO, AIG), 63
gross domestic product (GDP), 12,
    16, 17
  projected growth rates, 15
growth
  cost of, 15–18, 26–7

rate of, 5, 11, 12, 13, 15, 21, 26,
    27, 29, 31, 40
  see also economy
GDP *see* gross domestic product
GMAT exams, 111
Guan Zhong, 84–5
Guangzhou, 5, 8, 22, 60
guanxi, 36, 38, 48, 59–60, 61–70,
    89, 98, 99, 101, 103, 114, 117,
    118–19, 132, 137
  as banking, 70
  jiaren, 64
  king of (Vincent Lo), 62
  probational (of foreigners), 65–6
  problems with, 67–9
  shengren, 64
  shuren, 64, 65
  techniques for business, 67–70
  zijiren, 64–5
  see also family; friendship
guanxiwang (social network), 55
  see also networking

H
Haier, 20, 21, 30, 129
Han dynasty (206 BC–220 AD), 44,
    78, 81
Han ethnic/cultural group, 3
Hannibal, 112
harmony (*hexie/hemu*)
  see Confucianism
  social, 55, 62, 83
Heineken, 32
hexie/hemu (harmony)
  see Confucianism; harmony
hierarchy, 44–5, 46, 61, 62,
    83, 94, 99, 100, 125, 139,
    143
historical context, key differences
    between China and the West,
    139–40

history *see* cultural history;
    dynasties; Middle Kingdom
Hofstede, Geert, 123
homosexuality, 59
Honda, 18
Hong Kong, 4–5, 38, 72, 74, 125,
    131
Hong Lou Meng see *Dream of Red
    Mansions*
hong qi (red flag) limousines, 50
How to be a Good Communist, 57
Huai River, 15
huaqiao (overseas Chinese), 73–4,
    131
hukou (residential permit system),
    5, 59
husbands, 46, 47, 54, 65
    see also fathers

I
IBM, 110
IKEA, 38
illegitimate children *see sishengzi*
illness, 55–6
incomes, 5, 6, 7, 21, 31, 39
    disparities, 5, 15, 16, 76, 132
    disposable, 31
    'gold collar' workers, 7
    high, 7, 132
    low, 39, 73
    manufacturing, 21
    of foreign experts, 39
    other countries, 6–7, 38–9
    United States, 6
individuality, key differences
    between China and the West,
    140
Industrial and Commercial Bank of
    China, 23
initiative in business, 121, 127, 129
innovation, Chinese, 32, 33

inscrutability, 81–91
    see also communication; emotions
Intel, 110
intellectual property rights (IPR),
    35, 36, 106–10
    enforcement, 108
    and foreign companies, 108–10
    protection, 42, 108, 109–10
    violations, 108, 109, 110
    see also counterfeiting
International Energy Agency, 17
investment, high-tech, in China,
    110–11
IPR *see* intellectual property rights
'iron rice bowl', 20, 121, 133
Italy, 106

J
Japan, 7, 12, 18, 25, 27, 30, 38, 72,
    74, 75, 94, 95
    automotive industry, 112
Japanese
    prejudice against, 74–5
    prejudice of, 75
Jia Baoyu, 85
Jiang Zemin, President, 3, 4
jiaren (family), 140–1
    see also guanxi
Jinjiang Group, 20–1
Jiu, Prince, 84–5
jobs *see* labour
joint venture companies, 24, 40, 42,
    60, 63, 68, 69, 76, 83, 88, 89,
    90, 93, 98, 100, 120, 122, 126
Journey to the Middle Kingdom, 73
junzi (person of quality), 45, 56–7

K
Kelon, 20
Kingdom of Chi, 97
Kingdom of Wu, 94

King-Hall, Stephen, 1
King of the Children, 48
Kissinger, Henry, 65
Kodak, 31, 34
Kong Fuzi *see* Confucius
Korean war (1951–3), 72
Koxinga, 123
Kroll Associates, 107
Krugman, Paul, 13
Kuomintang, 95

L
labour
  cheap, 21, 22, 39, 116
  costs, 11, 12, 38–9
  market, 21
  wages, 21
  see also migrant workers;
    unemployment
Lan Luh Luh, 112
languages, 3, 81, 85, 126, 131
  spoken, 3, 4, 65, 67, 101, 117
  written, 4
  see also communication;
    Mandarin; Pinyin
Lardy, Nicholas, 25
laughter, 91
laws, 34, 35, 36, 57, 68, 107, 108
legal and regulatory framework, 32,
  36–7, 62
legal system, 37, 44, 61, 62, 86,
  119
Legend *see* Lenovo
Lei Feng, Good Soldier, 129
Lenovo computers, 20, 30, 31
Lever, 125
LG, 30
Li Lanqing (former Vice-Premier),
  68
Lin Biao, 44
Lin Daiyu, 85

'little emperor' generation
  see one-child policy
Little Red Book, 57
Liu Bei, 81–2
Liu Shaoqi, 50, 57
loans, *see* banking
Long March, 79

M
mainlanders, 74
Makro, 38
management, 2, 18, 20, 23, 33, 34,
  37, 39, 43, 68, 94, 98, 114,
  115, 121–34
managers, 18, 22, 24, 25, 48, 52,
  68, 74, 76, 81, 88, 100, 121,
  125, 126, 128, 129, 130, 131,
  132, 133
  expatriates, 22, 39, 52, 66, 76, 130
  retaining key local staff, 132–3
  sourcing, 131–2
  Western, 125, 126, 128, 129, 130
managing, 68, 124, 125, 127
  dilemmas, 124
Manchu, 60, 75,
Mandarin, 3, 4, 15, 126, 127
manipulation
  acquisition of information, 95
  deception, 95, 106
manufacturing, 13, 18, 21, 30,
  39–40
Mao Zedong, Chairman, 19, 20,
  27, 32, 44, 57, 78, 79–80, 95,
  107, 118, 123
  legacy of, 27
market, Chinese
  competitiveness, 30–2
  corruption, 105–6, 118
  ease of entrance, 29–32, 39–42,
    111–12, 115
  growth, 2, 11–27, 40, 116

knowledge, 137
labour, 5, 116
options, 39–40
segmentation, 7–9
size of, 5–7, 32, 40
test, 8
Western, 38, 112
marketing, direct, 37
marriage, 57, 59, 60, 85
Mary Kay, 37
Matsushita, 30
MBA, 34, 98, 114, 130
McDonnell Douglas, 69
meals *see* restaurants
meetings, business, 52, 90–1, 117
    addressing people, 90
    arrival times, 89
    asking questions, 90
    discontinuing to avoid conflict,
        101
    domination of Westerners in, 82
    dress code, 90
    formality in, 90
meltdown scenario, 14
Metro, 38
mianzi (face) *see* Confucianism
Microsoft, 110, 115
Microsoft China, 47
Middle Kingdom, 41, 77
migrant workers, 22
Ming dynasty, 77, 78, 79
mistresses, 76
    see also women
mobile phone sector, 12, 17, 30–1,
    40, 111, 113
modernisation, 43
moon festival, 51–2
Morgan Stanley, 21
mortgages, 23
Motorola, 30, 31, 32
Mulder, Mauk, 123

N
names, 90
National People's Congress, 36
negotiation, 93–104, 112, 116, 142
    see also restaurants
negotiation practices, 111
negotiation process, 98, 100–4
    exploration, 100, 101–2
    expectation structuring, 100, 102
    finalising, 101, 103
    perceptions and procedures, 104
    renegotiating contracts after
        signing, 103, 111
    solution building, 100, 102–3
nepotism, 133
networking, 42, 48, 52–3, 55, 62,
    63–4, 66, 67, 69, 70, 118, 132
    see also guanxi
Nike, 40
Ningbo Bird, 30
Nissan, 18

O
Olympic Games (2008), 29, 50
one-child policy, 6, 57–8, 64
'Open Door' policy (1978), 43–4
opium, 71–2, 79, 124
outsourcing, 40
overcapacity in sectors, 17–18
overseas Chinese (*huaqiao*), 73–4,
    131

P
Panasonic, 30
passport, applying for, 37
paternalism, 122, 125–6
    see also 'iron rice bowl';
        state-owned enterprises
payment, receiving, 38
Peng Dehuai, Marshall, 19
People's Republic, 27

person of quality *see junzi*
person, small (*xiaoren*), 57
personal space, 89
  see also physical contact
PetroChina, 18, 20
physical contact, 59, 89
Pinyin, 145–6
piracy *see* counterfeiting
Pittsburgh University, 19
politeness, 126
politics, 20, 24, 25, 27, 34, 41, 45,
  56–7, 78, 107, 108, 111, 121,
  122
pollution, 16
Polo, Marco, 1, 78
population, 3–10
  working in agriculture, 16
  growth, 5–6, 21
  middle class, 6, 12
  one-child policy, 6, 57–8, 64
  richest people, 16
  rural, 5, 21, 93
  size, 3, 5, 5–6, 8, 12, 22, 110,
    139
  unemployed, 21–2, 108
  United States, 6
  urban, 5
power distance, 123
power shortages, 17
prejudice
  against Chinese, 71, 76, 77
  of Chinese, 47, 53, 72, 73, 74,
    75, 94
  see also 'China bashing';
    xenophobia
pre-marital sex, 59
PricewaterhouseCoopers (PWC), 41
Procter and Gamble, 32
promotion, 76, 83
  missing out on, 60, 76
property development, 23

public safety, 16
Public Security Bureau, 35, 63
PWC *see* PricewaterhouseCoopers

Q
Qin Shihuang, 78
Qing dynasty (1644–1911), 60, 79,
  123, 145, 147
queueing, 89

R
Rape of Nanjing, 74
real estate, 17–18
R&D (Research & Development),
  32
regulations, 8, 23, 32, 34, 35, 36,
  37, 107, 108, 138
relationships
  living together, 59
  mixed couples, 60
  showing affection, 59
  see also family; *guanxi*
residential permit system (*hukou*),
  5, 59
restaurants, 49, 99, 125
  paying for meals (haggling), 52,
    67
  see also food
Rohmer, Sax, 91
Royal Institute for International
  Affairs, UK, 41

S
Sage of Qufu, 78
salaries *see* incomes
Samsung, 30
SASAC *see* State Assets Supervision
  and Administration Council
Second World War, 74
sexual revolution, 59–60
Shang dynasty, 77, 78, 79

Shanghai, 4, 7, 8, 16, 20, 22, 24, 29, 43, 58, 59, 60, 62, 69, 88, 89, 116
Sheffield University, library, 41
Shen Nong, 77
shuren see friendship
silence, 90–1
'silk road', 78
Singapore, 44, 131
Sino-Japanese war (1937–45), 72
sishengzi (children born outside marriage), 59–60
size of China, 4, 44, 108, 139
see also population
slowdown scenario, 14
Smith, John F. (CEO, GM), 63
social etiquette, 48, 51, 52, 56, 57, 94, 100
social harmony, *see* harmony
social network (*guanxiwang*), 55
see also guanxi; networking
social security system, 132
SOEs *see* state-owned enterprises
Software Publishers' Association, 106
Song dynasty, 33, 78
South Korea, 39
Soviet Union, border dispute with (1961), 72
space, personal, 89
Starbucks, 115
State Assets Supervision and Administration Council (SASAC), 18
state-owned enterprises (SOEs), 5, 6, 14, 18, 19–20, 22, 23, 24, 25, 33, 60, 69, 83, 89, 90, 93, 100, 103, 120, 121, 122
management model, 122
reforming/restructuring, 18, 19–21

steel, 17, 19
strategies, 114–18
see also 36 Strategies
Sui dynasty, 78
Sun Yat Sen (Sun Zhongshan), 79
Sun Zi, 78, 94, 95, 96, 112, 113, 114–15, 116, 133

T
Taiping rebellion, 79
Taiwan, 38, 39, 44, 74, 123, 131
Tang dynasty, 47, 78
TCL, 20, 30
teachers, 44, 47–8, 106, 113, 129, 140
team-working, 67–8, 128–9
television viewing, 8
theft from banks, 24, 120
Three Gorges Dam, 32
Three Kingdoms, 81–2
Tian, General, 97
Tiananmen, 26, 27, 79
Tianjin, 38
time, perception of, 43, 89
key differences between China and the West, 142
Toyota, 18, 32
Trade-Related Aspects of Intellectual Property Rights Agreement, 108
traffic gridlock, 16
Treaty of Nanjing, 72
Triads, 79
trust, relations of, *see guanxi*
Tsingtao Beer, 32

U
U2, 38
UK Trade and Industry, 42

unemployment, 21–2, 108
UNESCO, 17
universities
    China, 17, 59, 110–11
    United States, 110
United States, 131
    income, 6
    museum relics, 72
    population, 6
    universities, 110
'untrustworthiness' of Chinese
    business people, 105–20
US–China trade talks (2003), 72

V
Vanhonacker, Wilfred, 67
Vietnam war, 72
Vincent Lo, 62
Volkswagen (VW), 12, 18

W
wages see incomes
Wal-Mart, 12, 38, 40
Wang Corporation, 58
Wang, Dr An (Wang Corporation
    founder), 58
Warring States (476–221 BC), 96,
    97
Washington University, US, 37
Water Margin, 85
water supplies, 16
Watsons, 38
weddings, 43
Wee Chou Hou, 112
Westerners, 1, 2, 3, 4, 29, 30, 32,
    46, 47, 48, 49, 52, 53, 60, 64,
    65, 67, 72, 73, 75, 79, 88, 89,
    90, 91, 99, 100, 101, 102, 103,
    112, 113, 114, 118, 125, 126,
    139–43
    Chinese view of, 82

view of Chinese, 82
    see also expatriates; foreigners
Westernisation, 43–60
White Rabbit sweets, 32
Wholly Owned Foreign Enterprises,
    42
wives, 46–7, 56, 65
women, 47, 59–60, 77, 90
    see also concubines; mistresses;
        wives
'woofies' see Wholly Owned
    Foreign Enterprises
working for foreign companies,
    132–3
work units, 125–6
WorldCom, 130
World Exhibition, 29
World Trade Organization (WTO),
    20, 23, 32, 35, 108
Wu Jinglian, 13
Wu Shihong (former head of
    Microsoft China), 47
Wu Yi (China's Vice-Premier), 72
Wu Yi (WTO), 47
Wu Zetian, Empress, 47

X
xenophobia, 71–7, 101
    see also prejudice
Xia dynasty, 77
Xiabo, Prince, 84
Xian, 78
xiaoren (small person), 57
Xie, Andy (Morgan Stanley), 21
Xintiandi district, 62

Y
Yellow River, Huanghe, 16, 44
Yin and Yang, 53, 54–5, 94, 140
Young, Shirley, 63
Yuan dynasty, 78

Z
zijiren see friendship
Zheng, Duke of, 116
Zheng He, Admiral, 77

Zhou dynasty, 78, 116
Zhou Enlai (Premier), 5, 50, 63, 145
Zhou Zhengyi, 24
Zhu Rongji, 18, 34